Among the Repatriated

Among the Repatriated

Autobiography of a Mexican American

Albino R. Pineda

To order additional copies of this book, contact:
Xlibris Corporation
1-888-795-4274
www.Xlibris.com
Orders@Xlibris.com
44389

CONTENTS

Chapters

Dedication

I have written this memoir at the request of my children who wanted to know about my childhood and life as a young man. It is to them and my beloved late wife, Naomi, that I dedicate this book.

Acknowledgements

I am forever grateful to the following people who helped make this manuscript possible:

Mr. Raymond Rodriguez, History Professor Emeritus, Long Beach City College, for his advice and encouragement;

My children, John, Patricia and Paul, for reading and editing the manuscript; and

My brother-in-law, Robert M. Salas, for the cover art work which he sketched based on a memory I described to him.

Introduction

In writing one's autobiography, I have discovered that it is very difficult to distinguish between fact and fiction, especially when events are not recorded immediately. Many of the events experienced throughout our lives become blurry or totally forgotten. As I tried to remember events that I had experienced during my growing years, I was only able to capture nebulous fragments of what really happened. The rest I left to my imagination although we are told that all the experiences in our lives are stored in our subconscious.

Perhaps my children and grandchildren through their inquiries about particular events of my life have triggered and stimulated my subconscious to bring forth a relatively accurate accounting of those events. I have narrated the events of my life as they came to mind as well as those I carefully recorded in my personal diaries.

All in all, it has been a satisfying experience to capture the many experiences I have had throughout my long life which I believe are common to many Mexican-Americans.

Chapter I

MY PARENTS

My father, Emilio Pineda, was one of many Mexicans who came to the United States in 1917 to work on the railroads. Records show that in June of 1917, he registered with the U.S. Selective Service Office while a resident of Marfa, Texas, but he was never inducted into the armed services. Although my father was not a legal resident of the United States, he and thousands of other Mexicans were allowed to work in this country without fear of deportation because of a shortage of manpower during World War I. It was sometime around 1920 to 1921 that he met my mother, Dolores Rivera in Lordsburg, New Mexico, while working as a railroad laborer. Dolores and her brothers, Jose and Carlos, had crossed the border without documents. She and her brothers earned a living by building bird cages and bullhorn coat hangers, which they sold in the streets.

To this day, I have not found any records that show that Emilio and Dolores ever officially married. Quite possibly, their relationship was a common-law marriage. Soon after they became a couple, they moved to Phoenix, Arizona, where Emilio became a sharecropper on a small farm owned by a Mr. Hayden. Mr. Hayden spent a lot of time hunting and fishing in California and my father took care of his farm. The farm was located on Indian School Road. Emilio raised vegetables, watermelons, corn, and cotton. There was also an orchard on the farm with a variety of fruit trees.

Emilio and Dolores were living in a tent on the Hayden farm when Dolores gave birth to their first child, Elpidio. After Elpidio's birth, Emilio and Dolores found a one-room cabin on another farm about half a mile west of Mr. Hayden's farm. The cabin was owned by a Mr. Teal who allowed Emilio and Dolores to live in the cabin in exchange for Emilio's part-time work on the Teal farm. While working for Mr. Teal, my father also continued with his main job on the Hayden farm.

Shortly after my parents moved into the one-room cabin, I was born and my parents named me Albino after my maternal grandmother whose name was Albina. In the four succeeding years, they had two other sons whom they named Antonio and Isidro, with Isidro being the youngest.

In addition to her brothers, Jose and Carlos, Dolores had another brother, Inez, who became a police officer in Los Angeles, California. Her mother, Albina, lived in Riva Palacio, Chihuahua, Mexico. Her brother Jose worked at a nearby dairy, and Carlos had gone to work at a railroad yard in Los Angeles, California. Dolores also had three daughters by a previous union. They were all married. The oldest daughter, Luz, lived on a nearby farm. The middle daughter, Josefa, lived in a nearby mining town called Superior; and the youngest daughter, Dolores, lived in Santa Paula, California.

On Emilio's side, little was ever known about his family in part because of his premature death. The only thing known was that he had a sister who was a deaf-mute to whom he used to send clothing.

My Grandmother—Albina Barragan Rivera

Back row: my father - Emilio Pineda, my brother - Elpidio, my mother - Dolores; Front row: Albino and baby brother Antonio.

My Father - Emilio Pineda

Aunt Elena Rivera and Albino

Uncle - Carlos Rivera, Mother -Dolores R. Pineda, Uncle -Jose Rivera

Uncle - Inez Rivera

Sisters - Dolores Zavala and Josefa Rabago

Sister - Luz T. Chavez

Brother - Elpidio, Sister - Dolores Zavala, and Albino

Chapter II

MY BIRTH

As I previously mentioned, I was the second child born to Emilio and Dolores Pineda. Like my two younger brothers, I was born in the one-room cabin on the Teal farm, which was our only home during my father's life. My birth occurred on the morning of December 22, 1923. According to my oldest half sister, Luz, our family doctor, Coit I. Hughes, spent all night in our cabin waiting for my birth. To ward off the cold, he kept taking swigs from a whiskey bottle. When I was born, Calvin Coolidge was president of the United States and only a few weeks earlier, he had given his first annual message to Congress. Canada had issued an order forbidding American fishing vessels to enter Canadian harbors after December 31, except in an emergency. President Coolidge had just appointed Charles G. Dawes to head a committee to formulate a plan for defeated Germany's recovery. In sports, the New York Yankees had topped the New York Giants in the World Series. The average prices for various goods at the time were as follows: $0.09 for a loaf of bread, $0.56 for a gallon of milk, $295 for a new automobile and $7,400 for a new home. The average annual income was $ 2,126.

Chapter III

EARLIEST RECOLLECTIONS
OF MY LIFE

In my earliest recollections of my life, I remember being dragged as a baby through rows of a cotton field on top of a long sack tied to my mother's waist as she helped my father pick cotton. I still remember staring up and seeing tall cotton plants on both sides of the rows and the clear blue sky above. From that experience, I grew up thinking that cotton plants were at least six feet high when in reality they are only about three feet high.

I also remember sitting between my father and my mother on the seat of a one-horse buggy approaching a small wooden bridge in front of our cabin. The bridge was over a main irrigation ditch that ran along the south side of Indian School Road. On the edge of the ditch was a big evergreen tree. It provided shade in the hot summer, which we enjoyed. As we grew older, the irrigation ditch also provided a place for us to swim when the water was running.

As a three-year old, I remember running to one of my sister's arms every time a small airplane came flying by. I was terrified by the noise of airplanes. Small airplanes taking off from a nearby airport used to make a turn above our cabin. Sometimes, they would fly low and the pilots would wave at us.

As children, my brothers and I used to suffer from red-eye. When my mother put us to bed at night, she would apply eagle pomade to our eyes and tell us not to open our eyes until the next morning.

Another recollection is of me wearing pajamas with a buttoned flap across the rear end. One night, I felt the urgent need to relieve myself, but being a little kid I was frightened because the outhouse was about a hundred feet from our cabin and outside it was pitch dark. Somehow, I mustered the courage to go to the outhouse by myself in the dark but I hadn't walked very far when, all of a sudden, I felt something warm running down my legs. I can't remember what happened after that.

Chapter IV

MY EARLY CHILDHOOD

When I was around four years old, I began to get into all kinds of trouble. The big evergreen tree, next to the irrigation ditch, had a limb that hung over the ditch, and we used to swing from it and drop into the water when the irrigation water was running. If the ditch was dry, we would swing on the limb just for fun. One day, I went into the cabin without my mother seeing me and grabbed a handful of stick matches. I put them in one of the hind pockets of my Pay-Day overalls and went out to swing on the limb of the big evergreen. I grabbed the limb and swung very low in a circular motion. As I came around, my back pocket rubbed against the side of the ditch and the matches caught on fire. That was the last time I put matches in my pockets.

Another experience I recall is a day when I went out to play after lunch. I had a piece of tortilla, which I was eating. I decided to put the tortilla on the ground while I played with my brothers and after a while, I picked up the tortilla and continued to eat it. After a few bites, I felt a terrible sting in my stomach. It felt like someone had stabbed me with an ice pick. I began to cry out loudly, and throw up at the same time. As I looked at my vomit, I saw a red ant wiggling in the vomit. I hadn't noticed that it had been helping me eat my tortilla. I don't wish anyone such an experience.

As I grew older, my sense of curiosity kept getting me into trouble. One day, I went with my older brother to buy petroleum for our night lamp at the store next door to our cabin. On the way back, I picked up a cigar butt, took it home and lit it. I gave it a couple of whiffs and in a few seconds, our cabin began to go round and round, and I began to throw up. I staggered and fell to the ground. My mother came over and took me to bed thinking that I had experienced a *desmayo* (fainting spell). I was clearly learning everything the hard way.

The cabin we lived in was very small and situated about a hundred feet south from the road. Approximately, three years after I was born, my father built another small room about five feet from the entrance to the cabin. It was a crude-looking room made out of scraps of wood with a piece of canvass for a roof. The room became the kitchen and a bedroom for us kids.

South of our cabin was an alfalfa field, and at the far end was the Teals' home with a barn next to the Maricopa canal, which carried a lot of water. In the summer we went swimming in the Maricopa canal. We were very lucky that none of us drowned swimming in a big canal without supervision.

The Teal family had two adult children, Marvin and Mischa. I'm not sure I have spelled Mischa's name correctly, but that's the way it sounded to me phonetically. Marvin and Mischa milked the cows and did the chores associated with making butter.

To the west of our cabin were fields as far as the eye could see. The field right next to us was used to grow maize. I remember seeing Mr. Teal shooting a shotgun at flocks of birds that were eating the grain from the maize plants. Farther west was a hayfield. I recall my father picking up the hay and loading it on a wagon pulled by two mules. We would ride on top of the load of hay to the place where it was unloaded and stacked. I recall climbing on a stack and sliding down to the ground, which was fun for us kids.

Across the road from the cabin to the north were fields with different kinds of trees. We used to go into those fields to hunt for doves with slingshots. Near the road, the Johnson grass grew about five feet high. One day, we befriended an Indian boy from the Indian school who was older than we were. Together we hid in an area of grass where he tried to teach us how to smoke cigarettes. What we didn't realize was that my mother could see smoke rising from the grass. That adventure didn't last long.

My father, as I remember him, was a gentle person. He loved his children, and we loved him. When he came home in the evenings, tired from plowing, he would lie down on the bed to rest before dinner, and we would all lie on top of him. He clearly loved being with his children. However, my father was very strict when it came to misbehavior. One day, my older brother and I crossed under a barbed wire fence into the maize field to cut some cane, which we liked to chew on. On the way back, as we crossed under the fence, I held the barbed wire so my brother could cross. When I let the wire go, it hit him and scratched his neck, so he started to cry and ran to tell Dad. When I got home, I got belted. On another occasion, I recall my brother Tony and I each grabbed a nickel from some change that my dad had placed on a table. We went to the store and bought boxes of Cracker Jacks. When we got home, my mother asked us where we got the boxes of Cracker Jacks. That day, we got a spanking from my father for taking money without permission.

Another thing I remember of my early childhood is my mother sending my older brother Elpidio and me to sell hot tamales at the streetcar terminal across from the entrance to the Indian school. As people got off the streetcars, we would call out, "Hot tamales!"

I also remember taking a gunny sack and going to the rear of a bakery where the delivery trucks brought back the day-old bread that didn't sell. They would dump the bread into barrels. For a quarter, we could fill the sack with bread, cakes, and pies. Some of the bread and pastry were smashed but still edible.

Also, my uncle Jose, who worked at a nearby dairy, would bring us a gallon of chocolate milk every so often, which was a great treat for us.

My father used to bring home boxes of old clothes. I loved bell-bottom jeans and equestrian pants. The best outfit I ever remember getting was a new pair of shorts with a matching shirt. It had a belt with a leather strap that went up my right shoulder and down my back. I felt proud when I wore that outfit because I thought it made me look like a policeman.

I remember going to kindergarten and then first grade, which I don't think I ever finished. The name of the school was Osborn Elementary School, which was located about a mile south of Indian School Road on Central Avenue.

Our one-room cabin was behind a grocery store, which was at the corner facing Central Avenue. The owners of the grocery store were a Chinese family who had three kids similar in age to my brothers and me. I remember them washing their feet and putting on sandals every night before going into their house, which was part of the grocery store building. The three kids were the only kids around for miles.

The first automobile I remember us owning was an old convertible Model T. I recall seeing my father on cold mornings jacking up one of the rear wheels and lighting a small fire under the oil pan to facilitate cranking it. Today, I still wonder why the car never caught on fire. The second car I remember us owning was a four-door Model T. My father used to take out the back seat to accommodate boxes of fruits and vegetables, which he took to the market in downtown Phoenix. Dad used to like to go downtown to play hardball, or rebote as it was called.

Dad was not a man who came home drunk although on occasions, I would see Mr. Hayden share a drink with Dad as he was leaving for home after a hard day's work. The only time I remember seeing my father somewhat drunk was during a party at a nearby farm. I don't recall if it was at my sister Luz's house, but I do recall seeing my father very quiet with a half smile on his face, which told this little kid that he was feeling "high." That night, driving home along Indian School Road, we ran off the road into a drain ditch that ran along the road. Our car ended up leaning at a forty-five-degree angle, and the reason we didn't turn over was because the opposite side of the ditch held the car. That night, we walked the rest of the short distance to our house.

My mother was a harsh disciplinarian. One time, my nephew Johnny and I went to the store, and each of us took a lollipop without paying for them. When we got home, my mother saw us and immediately wanted to know where we got the candy. When we confessed, she told us we were not going out of the cabin for the rest of the day, and tied us to the foot of the bed.

My parents had a comadre who was my godmother by baptism, and we used to visit her home. I remember that she would always pick me up in her arms and kiss me, which I hated with a passion (typical kid).

My sister Luz and her family lived on a nearby farm until they decided to return to Mexico where they thought life would be better. They went to live in the state of Sinaloa, Mexico. Every so often, my half sister Dolores and her family would come from California to visit us.

I was in the first grade when my father got sick with a gallbladder infection. I remember that friends of our family tried some home remedies on him. They placed a fifty-cent coin on the area where he felt the pain, and put a small burning candle on the coin. Then they covered the candle with a glass jar. When my mother finally realized they weren't doing any good, she got hold of a doctor who immediately asked that my father be taken to the hospital. He was operated on right away for the removal of his gallbladder, and died three days later of peritonitis. I vividly remember my mother coming down the road from the streetcar terminal. We were playing under a tree, and as I saw my mother in the distance, I noticed that she was crying. I immediately concluded that something bad had happened. Next, I remember going to the county morgue to view my father's body before burial in the county cemetery. My father's body had been placed in a pine casket in the same condition it was in when he died. I viewed his body which was wrapped in a sheet and even as a small child, I could see the look of pain in his face. That has stayed with me throughout the years. As children, we were very traumatized by my father's premature death. I remember seeing my older brother crying, and wondering why I couldn't cry myself.

After my father's death, a man named Chris started to court my mother. When my older sister Josefa found out, she became furious. When Chris showed up the next time, she ran him off. She threw a glass gallon jar at him, and told him not to come back again. Even though my father was only a step-father to my three half-sisters, they loved him very much and always referred to him as Don Emilio.

Soon after my father's death, my mother sold some farm implements my father had owned, a couple of mules and our car. According to my brother Tony, we then moved away to somewhere nearby before our big move to Nogales, Mexico, where we would spend the rest of the Depression years and live until our late teens.

Brother - Antonio, Albino, Nephew - Johnny Chavez

Chapter V

OUR MOVE TO MEXICO

In the year of 1933, the Depression was in full swing and as a result, jobs became very scarce. My mother heard from others that the U.S. government was repatriating undocumented Mexicans, like her, back to Mexico. She became concerned that, at any moment, the immigration agents might come and ship us back to Mexico. Unfortunately, she decided we would go on our own. My sister Luz and her family were already in Mexico, and Luz had told my mother that life over there was cheaper. What she didn't tell my mother was that there were no jobs. All I remember about the journey to Mexico is riding in the back of a truck with my brothers and the few possessions we had. I don't recall that we knew where we were going although I do remember being excited because we were going on a long trip. Our most prized possessions were a bed with a copper head board, a Singer sewing machine, a late-model Victrola and my father's records which included all the waltzes of the time, and a large trunk that only my mother opened. I remember enjoying the ride as we sat on top of our possessions and the wind ruffled our hair in all directions. My mother was in the cab, and the driver of the truck was Chris, the man who had been courting my mother.

I don't recall arriving in Nogales, Arizona, but I do remember waking up the next morning in a garage where we spent the night in the truck. It was spring and I remember seeing a green hill a block away from where we had spent the night. It was a novelty to us because in Phoenix, we didn't have mountains or hills so near. I don't remember crossing the border into Nogales, Mexico, but do recall moving into a house with cement floors. That luxury was only temporary. My mother still had some money left from the sale of our car, the farm implements and the two mules, but as money began to dwindle, we were forced to downgrade our lifestyle, which wasn't that great to begin with. I enrolled in the second grade at a school that was on top of a hill. The name of the school was Francisco I. Madero. It turned out to be a traumatic experience for me because I only knew *pocho* Spanish which didn't help me very much. I remember that I had a very pretty teacher. She kept a glass of water on her desk, and every time she drank water from the glass, I would stare at her beautiful teeth as they became magnified by the glass.

Being in Mexico was very foreign to me. We were accustomed to living on a farm isolated from people except for the Chinese family who lived in the store next to our cabin. Living in Nogales, Mexico, was a different world, full of neighbors along narrow streets where kids would play. There were also mountains and canyons nearby which did not exist in Phoenix. We learned to adapt to our new environment.

My brothers and I were known as *los repatriados* (the repatriated), a label that was used for kids who were victims of the repatriation. I had never lived near so many kids. People lived along the hillsides. Vendors sold fruits and all kinds of goods in the streets and from house to house. Some carried large milk cans and sold milk by pouring it into containers the customers had to provide. Very early in the morning, men carrying portable tables on their heads would call out, "Pan, pan, panadero!" as they sold freshly baked bread in the hillside neighborhoods.

Also foreign to me was seeing a funeral procession with mourners walking behind a horse-drawn hearse.

I recall a heavy set man with a deformed hand going from house to house begging for handouts. It seemed that every time he came knocking on our door, he would have a seizure and fall toward the inside of the house as soon as we opened the door. Later on, we began to realize that he did it deliberately to draw attention. He was known in the neighborhood as El Cinco Pansas (the Five-Belly Man).

A few months later, we moved to a canyon known as La Canada Vasquez, which was a tough neighborhood. We lived in a one-room apartment with wooden floors. We had a neighbor a few doors down from us who would get drunk and fight with his adult son who was also drunk. A crowd of neighbors would gather to watch them fight. The woman of the house used to do ironing and always had a can with hot coals outside the house to heat the iron. As the father and son fought each other, the crowd watched with interest to see which of the two would end up on top of the hot coals.

On other occasions, we would see a big crowd of people coming up the street, with two men leading the crowd to a place outside of the neighborhood to engage in a fist fight.

It wasn't unusual to see men or women engaged in a fist fight in the middle of the day. Once, I saw two women rolling around on the ground, hitting each other and pulling at each other's hair.

On another occasion, I saw a duel between two Mexican soldiers who engaged in a really bloody fight. They cut each other into a bloody mess, using pieces of broken glass. It was a duel in the rain, and nobody in the crowd would call the police. Living in this poor neighborhood resulted in our witnessing many frightful things that, in time, became a part of our everyday life.

Eventually, my sister Luz and her family moved from the state of Sinaloa to Nogales. She lived across town in a canyon known as Canada Buenos Aires. She had a knack for cooking and always worked in restaurants. She was always concerned about our well-being. Sometime later, she had marital problems, and her husband left her to join the Mexican Army. He never saw his children again. After he left, we moved next door to Luz's house. By then, we were among the poorest of the poor. I remember that the son of my nephew's godmother asked me to go begging with him in the downtown area. I told him I would go if he did the begging. He said he would, so I went with him. I remember him saying to passers-by, "Una moneda por el amor de Dios!" We never got anything. People in those days didn't have any money to give. Beggars were on every corner.

The house we moved into next to Luz's house was a large one-room, adobe-walled house with a dirt floor. The house had an outhouse that was located behind the house on a hillside. In the back of the house was a one-room shack with parts of the walls missing. The shack was used as a bedroom for my brothers and me. I recall one morning waking up and looking up toward the ceiling and seeing a green snake coiled on one of the rafters. From then on, I slept in the main room where my mother slept for I was terrified of snakes.

Just beyond the shack was a well that provided our drinking water. The well had a crank that turned a shaft. A rope was tied to the shaft so we could lower a bucket into the well to get our drinking water.

We didn't live in that house very long because my mother rented another one-bedroom, wooden framed house that had a makeshift kitchen in the back. The wooden walls had big gaps between the boards, which we covered with nailed pieces of cardboard to keep the cold wind from blowing in. It was the last house in the outskirts of the neighborhood.

Beyond our house was a flat area, which we called El Llanito (the Little Plain), where we played baseball. Our bats were made out of tree limbs, and our gloves were made of canvas. We also made our own baseballs by wrapping pieces of string over small rubber balls.

From El Llanito to the east, there was nothing but low rocky hills with scattered yucca plants and cacti. There was a walking trail that went eastward for many miles to a place known as Mascarenas. It was a valley with many small farms. Most of the farmers had to fight to survive, raising small crops of corn and beans. Their homes, which were built of tree branches, were plastered with mud, all a reflection of their poverty. To the north of our house, about a quarter of a mile, was the U.S. border which was marked by a barbed wire fence.

Eventually, I started attending the neighborhood grammar school. The school, which still stands today, was called Escuela Enrique Quijada. It was a kindergarten through sixth grade school housed in a two-story brick building on top of a hill that had a view of the border and most of Nogales, Arizona. I had to start all over in the first grade. Fortunately, I had a good teacher. She was an elderly lady who was very dedicated to teaching. I wasn't there very long because I got transferred to the fourth grade, most likely, because of my height as opposed to my intelligence. In the fourth grade, my teacher was Senorita Carmen Villanueva, an attractive, young woman with whom I found favor. I was elected class representative for all the functions that took place in other schools.

The sidewalk in front of the school was about two feet high above ground level, and the school grounds were very rocky. Sharp rocks protruded from the ground, and most of us ran around barefoot. It wasn't unusual for some of us to go around limping because of injured toes or blisters on the soles of our feet. One time, I was running and jumping off the high sidewalk, when the heel of my right foot landed on a sharp rock that was sticking out from the ground. I ended up with a blister that was almost the size of a golf ball.

The basketball court was just as bad with sharp rocks sticking out from the ground, but that didn't keep the kids from playing basketball.

I recall Don Miguelito, a short man who was the school's truancy officer. He would walk up and down the steep hillside of the neighborhood rounding up kids, like myself, who were skipping classes. Some of us became very skillful at dodging Don Miguelito who carried a belt in his hands at all times. Unfortunately, because I needed to fend for myself in order to survive, I began to regularly miss school until I quit altogether.

Chapter VI

MY PRETEENS

My mother had a comadre who would buy American goods and take them to nearby ranches to sell or trade for homemade cheeses, beans, and other goods. She would take the traded goods to town to sell. The comadre and her husband, who was a cowboy type, owned a two-horse-drawn wagon. The wife would take the wagon to visit other ranches. Once, she took me along, and we stayed with some friends. The friends were a very poor family who barely survived on what they farmed. I've never forgotten the occasion. That evening, they invited us to a dinner that consisted of a small bowl of boiled beans. When we finished eating, the man of the family said, "If you didn't fill up (your stomach), there's a barrel of water. Fill yourselves up."

On several occasions, I went on trips with the husband of my mother's comadre who would go into the hills to get wood to sell in town. We would leave at noon and spend the night under a big oak tree by the side of the road halfway to our destination. Early the next morning around dawn, we would round up the horses, hook them to the wagon, and be on our way. On the way back, we would spend the night under the same oak tree. The husband, Mr. Duarte, was one of those macho men with a mean streak. On the return of one of our trips, we arrived at his house with a load of wood, but could not go in because his wife had forgotten to remove a chain that ran across the yard of the house. Just because his wife had forgotten to remove the chain, he jumped off the wagon in a rage, took the chain off the ocotillo fence, and yelled at his wife to come out. When she did, he began to whip her with the chain. The poor woman just kept saying, "I didn't realize you were coming so soon."

I remember another incident that occurred when I was returning with Mr. Duarte to his house via a narrow road. A man in another wagon came from the opposite direction. Neither the man nor Mr. Duarte made an effort to yield the right-of-way, so they began to argue, and Mr. Duarte pulled a gun on the other man. The man had no choice but to yield. On the next trip, by sheer coincidence, they met again. This time the road was a little wider and as they passed each other, the other man called out, "Are you going to pull a gun on me again?" For a moment, I thought I was going to find myself in the middle of a gunfight. Fortunately, nothing happened, and we continued on our way.

On another occasion, we were on our way to get a load of wood, and he let me ride one of his horses, which was a very skinny horse. On the way over, I fell way behind his wagon, and came to a railroad crossing that was elevated from the level of the road. As I reached the top and started to descend, I began to kick the horse with my heels because I wanted to catch up with the wagon. As the horse began to run down the grade, it tripped, fell forward and sent me flying. I landed on my belly. As I lay there stunned, I looked back and saw the horse kicking its legs up in the air trying to get up. Finally, the horse got up and so did I. After we both shook ourselves off, I remounted. I was glad that Mr. Duarte had not seen what had happened. However, upon remounting, I discovered to my horror that the iron head of the saddle was badly bent. *Now,* I thought, *what am I going to tell Mr. Duarte?* When he finally saw the bent saddle head, he immediately asked me how it got bent. I told him, "I didn't know," which was a dumb answer because no one had ridden the horse but me. For a moment, I thought that he was going to pull his gun on me too, but he didn't.

It seemed that I was having one bad experience after another. One day, I borrowed the same horse, and rode it to the opposite side of town just to prove to others that I could ride a horse. I decided to go by the slaughterhouse where we would pick up bladders from slaughtered cattle and blow air into them to make a football. To get to the slaughterhouse, I had to follow a dirt road that went under two sets of railroad tracks. The road went up a steep grade, and as one went up the road, the space between the road and the tracks narrowed.

Somehow, the saddle got caught on a railroad tie and the horse couldn't move forward or backward. Worst of all, my left leg got caught in between the saddle and the tie. There was no letting the air out of the tires or telling the horse to squat down. Fortunately, I was able to wiggle my leg out and drop to the ground. Next, I loosened the saddle strap and guided the horse backward until the saddle dropped to the ground. After giving a sigh of relief, I re-saddled the horse and headed back to the house.

That wasn't the end of my horse experiences. The last trip I took with Mr. Duarte is to be remembered for the rest of my life. Now, I think it is funny but at the time, it wasn't. We were on a narrow and curvy steep grade with a heavy load of chopped wood. I was sitting on top of the load of wood, which was quite high. The wagon was being pulled by two horses. The brakes consisted of a wood beam that ran under the wagon from side to side near the rear wheels. Attached to each end of the beam was a short vertical block of wood with a piece of rubber tire nailed to it. On the right side of the wagon seat was a long lever that, when pulled, would draw the blocks of wood and rubber against the rear wheels of the wagon. Those were the brakes. As we came down the steep grade, Mr. Duarte began to pull hard on the lever to activate the brakes because the heavy load was beginning to slide towards the horses. He hadn't realized that he had overloaded the wagon. He pulled so hard on the brakes that one of the brake blocks broke loose, and the wagon began to push up against the horses to the point that they panicked and took off running downhill. As we picked up speed around the curves of the narrow road, I could feel the load of wood swaying from side to side, with me sitting on top. By the grace of God, no cars or wagons were coming up the grade. Otherwise, I wouldn't be here writing this book. When we reached the bottom of the grade, we were probably traveling forty miles an hour. It took about a mile before the horses finally came to a stop. That was the end of my trips with Mr. Duarte.

At home, my mother realized that she couldn't provide for her children adequately, so she became easily frustrated and angry. As I mentioned earlier, the walls to our house were made of boards nailed vertically with large cracks between them, which allowed the cold winds to filter through. At night, we slept on the ground on top of a straw mat and when we got up in the morning, especially during the summer, we had to shake the mat to make sure that scorpions hadn't spent the night with us. Unfortunately, scorpions and snakes were very much a part of the environment.

My brothers and I took turns getting up early in the morning to light the wooden stove in our little kitchen. One of my jobs was to haul water from the well for drinking, cooking, and washing. There was a common well about a quarter of a mile from where we lived. I would carry water from the well in two five-gallon cans slung from a pole that I put across my shoulders. During the summer, the well would go dry, and users of the well would take turns going down to the bottom of the well to clean it. We would remove the frogs and dig the well a little deeper. The well was in a low area, so when it rained, it would flood and fill with debris and cow dung, which we had to clean out. Today, I look back and am amazed at how we drank dirty water without getting sick.

The other responsibility my brothers and I had was to go to the nearby hills to get wood for the stove. The hills around the city were mostly bare of trees or bushes of any kind. Anything that could be burned was chopped down. When wood wasn't available, dry cow dung burned well in the stove. The few ocotillo plants that grew nearby were cut down to make fences around the houses. In those days, no one seemed to care about the environment. Survival was what mattered. One could see a clear difference between one side of the border and the other. To the north, there were many trees, mostly mesquite and green brush; and to the south, the hills were almost completely bare of vegetation or trees.

We had a neighbor who lived nearby who worked as a janitor in a large grocery store downtown. Once a week, he would bring a pickup truck full of trash and sweepings from the store to a dump in El Llanito. He would sweep the floors of the store during the week, and sweep any beans that had dropped onto the floor into the trash. Some of our neighbors raised pigs for slaughtering, and would let the pigs roam around the homes in the neighborhood. Sometimes, the pigs would enter homes and eat anything they could find. Somehow, the pigs always knew when the neighbor had arrived with his truckload of trash for they would all run to the dump at El Llanito. When the neighbor would drive by with the trash, my mother would tell us to go and pick up as many beans as we could find. That became a competition between the pigs and us. The beans we collected were used to make the meal for the day.

I recall one time when a truck brought a load of rotten tomatoes. My mother gave us each a pot and a knife to cut the rotten parts off the tomatoes so she could cook the good parts. That night, we had boiled tomatoes with sugar for dinner. The interesting part is that in spite of our poverty, we were a bunch of happy kids.

In her desperation, my mother developed a relationship with a man she thought would be able to help her provide for the family. When she discovered that he was unable to contribute much, he was gone. Frustrated, my mother developed a mean streak.

One morning, she was outside doing the wash, stirring clothes with a broomstick in a tub of boiling water. I walked by, and don't recall what I said or didn't do, but I do recall that she hit me across the back with the broomstick. I fell to the ground and pretended that I had passed out so she would not hit me again. As I lay on the ground, she said, "Oh, so you passed out, huh? I'll revive you in a hurry," and she hit me again. I jumped up, and limping, I took off running as fast as I could to get away from her. One could not run away from my mother and get away with it. This happened in the morning; and as I ran, she yelled, "You'll pay for running away from me!" I ran to a nearby hill and stayed there most of the day. Even though the sun was very hot, I didn't dare come down from the hill. As the afternoon wore off, I began to slowly descend toward the house. I could see my brothers and nephews playing in the yard. Little by little, I began to approach the house and finally, got to where they were playing and joined them.

As evening approached, my mother came out to say that dinner was ready. Everyone went in, but I hesitated. Then, my mother came out and called me to come in and have dinner. I went in and sat at the table with the rest. Mother came and gave each one of us a tortilla, and then she started to serve us small bowls of boiled beans. When she got to me, she grabbed the back of the suspenders of my Pay-Day coveralls to make sure I couldn't run away, and said, "We have something to settle before you start eating." Without letting go of my suspenders, she reached for a belt she had hung by the door, and gave me a good belting; and every time she would hit me, she would say, "This is so you won't run away from me again." As soon as she stopped belting me, she told me to sit down and eat my beans.

As my mother aged and I grew up, her temperament softened and she developed a great deal of respect for me. I never lost respect for her. Towards the end of her life, she became a very concerned and loving mother. As I look back, I can now understand her frustration—the sudden death of my father and having four active boys for whom she could not adequately provide. She was an illiterate woman with no formal schooling of any kind in the middle of the Depression. It was a time when even those with a formal education could not find employment. Also, Mexico was not the place to live during those hard times.

There is a Christmas Eve that I have never forgotten. It's an experience I have shared with my children and grandchildren. I remember going to town hoping to run errands for someone to earn a few coins. I was always hungry and never had enough to eat. As I walked through downtown, I saw a big grocery store with a long counter full of customers buying the essentials for their Christmas meal. There were several clerks behind the counter, and I noticed that when people bought something, they were given a bag of cookies and *pilon* (candy) as an incentive to come back. So my mind began to work on how I could get that gift, too. The desire was so strong that I contrived a plan. I found a paper grocery bag and went looking for some small round rocks that resembled potatoes. I had no trouble finding a dozen, and put them into the paper bag. I went into the store and worked my way through the crowd of customers, and placed the bag on the counter. When a clerk came by, I told him that I had just bought some potatoes and wanted my pilon. He told me to ask the clerk that had taken care of me. I tried the same trick with three other clerks and got the same response. By then, I knew that my trick wasn't going to work. Discouraged, I worked my way through the crowd, went outside, and dumped the rocks. I then headed back home. I knew that there was no food at home, but nevertheless, I decided to go home.

As I walked home, I noticed that there was excitement everywhere. People who could afford things were busy buying food and gifts. I kept hearing a voice inside that kept telling me, "You are a poor child. You can't have anything. Poor children don't deserve nice things." Believing that, I continued to walk home. I passed my sister Luz's house and then decided to go back to her house, which was a one-room adobe building. The door and window of her house were covered with canvas that was rolled up during the day. At night, the canvas was rolled down to keep the cold wind from blowing into the dirt-floor room. Inside, my sister's stove consisted of a grill on top of some rocks. The grill itself was made from the top of a metal barrel. For kitchen cabinets, she had nailed some orange crates together. That was the house where I had seen my baby nephew Raulito die of fever. I still remember my sister Luz grabbing dirt in her hand and rubbing his eyes to close them.

When I arrived at my sister's house, I began to play with my nephews Johnny and Amador and my niece Dora. Being that it was Christmas Eve, I decided to stay for the night. They had a bed which consisted of a straw mat and a large heavy canvas for the bedspread. They kept the fire underneath the grill burning to provide heat. That night as we were getting ready to crawl under the canvas, one of my nephews suggested that we hang a stocking on the crates so Santa Claus could place some goodies in it while we slept. We found an old stocking that we hung on the crates, and went to bed feeling very excited. The next morning, we woke up really early and the first thing we thought about was the stocking. We all went to check the stocking and found it just like we had left it—empty. As we were innocent children, we gave Santa a way out. Our comments were "Maybe Santa Claus forgot to stop by" or "Perhaps he ran out of goodies."

Behind my sister's house was a road that went up a steep canyon. On Christmas morning, we heard kids' voices yelling and laughing, so we went outside and found a bunch of kids riding down the steep grade in their new wagons and bicycles. They were mostly children of merchants who could afford to buy their children toys. We sat on big rocks that were by the road to watch the kids enjoy their wagons and bicycles hoping that as the morning wore off, they would get tired of playing and allow us to ride their wagons down the grade. They never got tired, but at least, we enjoyed watching them have fun.

In those days, we had to learn to make our own toys. I built a wagon out of a wooden box. I found axles from wagons that had been discarded, and using a two-by-four, I built a nice wagon that I could also ride down the grade. I also learned to roll a metal ring along the road by guiding it with a stiff wire with a hook at the end. The other toy we enjoyed was an old car steering wheel that we found. We would hold the steering wheel in our hands, and pretend that we were driving a car by imitating the noise of a car with our voices. We would go up and down trails pretending that we were driving a car. As crude as our toys were, we enjoyed them a great deal.

The other thing I remember doing since we could not afford to buy shoes was to look for discarded old shoes. I would tear the old soles out, and look for a discarded rubber tire. Then I would nail the old shoes to a piece of rubber tire that I had cut to fit the shoes and my feet. The first time I did this I was able to wear shoes after not having worn shoes in a long time. I remember looking back at my footprints on the ground, and seeing part of the letters of Goodyear molded into the ground. It wouldn't have been difficult for someone to track me down. Interestingly, when I think about my childhood as hard as it was, I think about the beautiful experiences my brothers and nephews and I had as we were growing up.

As I grew a little older, I remember going to night school sporadically. I learned enough math to be able to add, subtract, divide, and multiply. And I could read and write enough to get by.

When I was about twelve years old, I began chopping wood for neighbors to earn a few cents. I still have a scar on one of my fingers from a piece of wood that flew off the log and cut my finger. Later on, I tried selling cream-filled pastries by walking up and down hilly neighborhoods. After walking all day long, I would earn about fifty centavos, which was the equivalent of ten cents in U.S. currency.

One day, the neighborhood barber asked me if I wanted to work for him. He wanted me take care of his cows. My job would be to go out early in the morning to the nearby hills to find the cows and bring them in for milking. The pay was fifty cents a day and meals. That was my first real job. At the time, I was wearing the most beautiful pair of tight, soft leather boots I had ever had. I don't recall how I acquired them, but I remember that I kept them very well shined. I accepted the job and after two weeks of walking up and down hills chasing cows, I developed a corn on my right foot that has bothered me for most of my adult life and I ruined my beautiful boots. One day, I brought the cows in, and I heard the barber's wife call me with a desperate voice. She was frantic because her four-year-old boy had a high fever and was delirious. She picked him up in her arms, and the little boy gave a jerk and died. I didn't know what to do, so I ran to tell her husband who then rushed home. I believe this job only lasted for about three weeks.

On another occasion, a nearby neighbor came over and told me that he could speak to spirits and get messages. He would place a sheet of paper on a small wooden table and press the tip of a pencil onto the paper, and then claim that a spirit had guided his hand to write a message on the paper. On one occasion, he allegedly spoke to the spirits and received a message on the paper. The message said that there was a buried treasure on one of the mountains that formed the canyon where we lived. He then gathered other neighbors, mostly adults, and me and we went to the mountain at midnight to dig for the buried treasure. I recall digging by candlelight and hearing this guy talking to the spirits while we dug a well six feet in diameter and about fifteen feet deep. We found no treasure. The spirits then allegedly told our neighbor through additional written messages to go to another nearby mountain. Like a fool, I believed it and went to help dig another deep hole on top of another hill. I remember pulling out a lot of loose rocks. Today, I wonder what kept the walls of the well from caving in on us. Finally, it dawned on me that this was weird stuff, so after several nights of digging, I gave up. That was one of the weirdest things I have ever done in my whole life. However, I suppose that when an adult tells a dirt-poor and ignorant kid that there's a treasure buried someplace, the kid will believe the adult.

My life was full of adventures as a young kid, with more to come. As a young boy, I used to roam the nearby hills looking for wild onions to eat. One day, I was on top of a hill looking down below at the town hospital. In front of the hospital, was a covered patio-like structure that was used as a holding station for coffins that were filled with dead people and were ready to be picked up by a horse-drawn hearse. As I looked down at the hospital, I became conscious of a light wind that had a very melancholic sound, which brought a sense of sadness to me. Since then, every time I hear and feel the summer wind blow, it takes me back to that occasion. Later on, after World War II, I read a story written by the late war correspondent Ernie Pyle in which he mentioned the melancholic sounds of the Midwest summer winds. I remember knowing exactly what he meant.

Up until the early forties, a common sight at the border was the arrival of hundreds of Mexican families who were being repatriated back to Mexico. The irony of it all was that out of every family of six, four were American citizens. Children of all ages had no choice but to come south *among the repatriated*. Most of the families that were deported, found themselves displaced without jobs. Most of them would move south to the state of their origin in hopes of living a better life. Those that stayed in Nogales, Mexico, learned to survive like we did. The community of *repatriados* began to grow, and those of us who were American citizens began to get passports so we could walk across the border to look for work.

A large family of repatriados moved near where we lived. The family consisted of the parents and eight children. Among the children was a married son, an adult daughter and a daughter about my age, who was very pretty. Her name was Carmelita. I remember having a crush on her, but I never had the courage to ask her out for a date. I guess it was my lack of experience and naivete. Later on, I experienced an embarrassing situation that involved her. She had met a fellow who had become her boyfriend. One evening, I bumped into her at the plaza and out of the blue, she asked me if I wanted to walk with her. It was the custom in those days for young people to walk around the plaza and a few blocks up along the main street and back. That was the pastime back then as there was nothing else to do. Anyway, Carmelita asked me to walk with her. What I didn't know was that she had experienced a spat with her boyfriend who was probably in a nearby cantina, and she wanted to make him feel jealous. I walked with her, and fortunately, we never came across the guy. The embarrassing part came as we reached the plaza again. Along the sidewalks, there were vendors selling sodas, fruits, and fruit drinks. I had a friend who managed one of the booths where different snacks were sold. As we walked by my friend's booth, she suggested that we have a soda. I said, "Of course," and we got the drinks. As I stuck my hand into my pocket, I discovered that I didn't have a cent. I said, "You know something, I don't have any money with me." (To be honest, I was always broke) She opened her purse, and she was also broke. If there was ever an embarrassing situation, this was it! Fortunately, my friend was at the booth and I told him I would pay him later. I never did go out with Carmelita again as much as I admired her.

Carmelita's family was as poor as my family. I remember going with her father and brothers to get firewood for their home. Her father had an old four-door Model T, and like my father, he would take the back seat out to accommodate the wood. Sometimes, all we could find were dried-up stumps. He would wrap a chain around a stump and pull it out with his car. Every time we came to a grade, we had to get out of the car and push the car uphill. I think that's why he always wanted us to go with him!

Albino's Passport for crossing the Border

Chapter VII

MY TEENS

As I grew into my teens, I discovered that freight trains bound for the United States, transporting fruits or tomatoes, always replenished the refrigerated cars with ice on the Mexican side before crossing the border. The old ice was dropped along the tracks. In those days, people used iceboxes to store their food so I saw the chunks of melting ice by the tracks as a potential means of income. After securing a couple of customers who agreed to buy ice from me, I carried an ice pick with me, carved big square pieces of ice and carried them on my back to make deliveries. I only made about fifty cents, which was enough to buy something to eat. I found that making ice deliveries could sometimes lead to serious consequences. A steady female customer of mine had a huge dog, which was always asleep in the kitchen where I made my deliveries. Every time I went in, the dog would raise its head, look at me, and go back to sleep. That was until one morning. On that morning, I went in and put the ice in the ice box. As I was opening the kitchen door to leave, I heard something heavy sliding across the wooden floor. Before I could look back, I felt the jaws of the heavy dog grab my right ankle. Fortunately, he didn't bite me. He just grabbed my foot and wouldn't let go until the woman came and pulled him back. From then on, I made sure that the woman was around before I went in.

Another incident occurred when I was going to deliver a piece of ice to a new customer in a different neighborhood. It was one of those brutally hot summer days. I had the heavy piece of ice tied to my back, and as I entered the new neighborhood, two kids—one about my age and the other a bit younger—wanted to take my chunk of ice. I told them where they could find all they wanted, but nope, they wanted my piece of ice. I wasn't about to let them have it. They began jerking me around, and soon, we were engaged in a fierce fight. We fought viciously for about ten minutes, and as the fight progressed, I began to feel the load on my back getting lighter by the minute. Finally, the fight ended suddenly because my attackers realized there was nothing left to fight for, and I realized I had nothing to defend. They went their way, and I went back to the source to get another piece of ice. That fight was one of the two fiercest fights I have ever had in my entire life.

The other fight took place near where I lived. There was a tall kid who always wanted to pick a fight with me. We were two of the tallest kids in the neighborhood, and he wanted to prove that he could whip me. I had heard that he wanted to fight me, but somehow, I had managed to avoid a confrontation. That is, until one day when I saw him waiting for me at the top of a grade as I was nearing home. With him were a bunch of other kids eagerly waiting for the excitement of a fist fight. The moment I saw him, I was overcome with fear. I sensed something ominous coming, yet I was determined to face whatever was coming my way. As we met, another kid ran up to me to place a piece of wood on my shoulder and said to my opponent, "Let me see you knock this piece of wood off his shoulder". The remark was meant to be an insult to which I was supposed to respond. Not only did he knock the piece of wood off my shoulder, but he also shoved me backward at the same time. That got us started with a big crowd of kids yelling wildly. My opponent and I were wearing straw hats, which everybody wore because of the hot sun. We started fighting and throwing windmill punches at each other. After about ten minutes of vicious fighting, we got tired and stopped. After we each surveyed the damage sustained by the other, we discovered that the only damage done was to the front of our hats. Our hats saved our faces. Satisfied that he had finally fought me, the guy never bothered me again.

I began hanging around the railroad yard with other kids from the neighborhood, and one day, I got a job washing and polishing the Pullman dining car silverware. I would wash it and then polish every spoon, fork, and knife. I was paid fifty cents for doing that.

Later on, I got commissioned to make ice cream for the dining car on the morning of the train's departure, which would occur in the afternoon. Every time I made ice cream, I would do it on the vestibule outside the dining car and there was always a bunch of kids asking for a taste. American tourists would arrive in Nogales, Arizona, and the Pullman car was pulled across the border, and hooked to the train bound for Guadalajara and Mexico City. After the Pullman was connected to the Mexican train, the evening meal was ready to be served in the dining car.

My brothers, nephews, and I discovered that Pullman porters, conductors, and other crew members always paid to have their luggage taken to the nearby hotels where they usually lodged. That became another source of income for us. It was a matter of nickels and dimes, which wasn't much, especially in Mexican currency, but at least we had a few cents in our pockets.

Trains would leave every other day except on weekends. I remember us hanging on to the passenger trains as they left. We would dare one another to see who could hang onto the train the longest as it picked up speed. We would also run from the top of freight trains from one car to the other on as many cars as we could.

One time, the new governor of the state of Sonora was going to be inaugurated, and a freight train was made available to anyone who wanted to go to the inauguration in the state capital of Hermosillo. Since it was a free ride, some of my friends and I decided to go. The long train was full of people, and I remember climbing on top of one of the boxcars. Halfway over, a kid decided to climb down one of the ladders on the side of the boxcar as the train was going full speed. What he didn't see was a spigot from a water tank that supplied water to the engines which was just inches from the passing cars. When he saw it, it was too late. It threw him in between the cars and down under. I remember looking down, and seeing his head roll under the wheels. I turned the other way in horror.

When we got to Hermosillo, it was so hot and muggy that I didn't go to see the inauguration. Instead, I remember going to a river to cool off. I can't recall what we did after that and whether we stayed overnight.

Nogales, Mexico, was an interesting border town with its Model T pickup trucks that served as *tranvias* (trolley cars). They had benches on both sides along the back of the truck with a roof on top. The tranvias ran from one end of the town to the other along the main drag, and for five centavos, you could ride across town. Silver was plentiful and cheap in those days. All along Calle Elias, curio shops with different kinds of silver jewelry catered to American tourists, and the main attraction was a restaurant in a cave that went deep into a rocky hill. There, diners were entertained by a mariachi band and singers.

We stayed away from that street because it was for the upper class people. Today, I recognize how shy I have been throughout my life. As a young man, not only was I shy but also insecure as well. Perhaps it was because of the deprivation and uncertainty I experienced as I grew up.

There used to be an annual festival in Nogales, Mexico. It was similar to the carnival they have in Rio de Janeiro. If you wanted to be part of the festival, you had to wear a *guayavera* (a costume and a mask). It was customary to change the pitch of your voice when wearing the mask so no one would recognize who you were. I remember attending a carnival where one of my friends and I decided to wear a costume and mask. We went to a honky-tonk dance that evening and even with the mask on, I was so self-conscious that I could not say hi to girls.

Chapter VIII

MY LATE TEENS

As a teenager, I was very tall and mature for my age. I remember that most of my friends were older fellows—in fact, some of them were married. We would drink beer and play pool two or three nights a week, especially on weekends. On one occasion, my friends and I were invited to a party where they were serving mescal—an almost-raw alcohol. I must have had one too many because I woke up the next morning lying on the floor with my head in between the legs of a chair. That was the beginning and the end of my drinking hard liquor. I was fortunate that my body would tell me when I couldn't handle any more to drink.

Being a tall kid who associated with grown-ups, I was invited to join a civic organization called Legion de Jovenes Mexicano (Mexican Youth League). We were taught how to march and execute certain maneuvers so we could participate in parades. We had a drum and bugle unit. We also used to help direct traffic. The organization became a source of discipline and fun since all my friends were also members. The only thing I didn't like was our heavy navy blue wool uniforms, especially during hot days. I lasted about a year and then dropped out. A funny thing I remember is that Mexican national elections were so lax that I, as an under-aged American citizen, was allowed to vote for a presidential candidate. I voted for General Juan Andreu Almazan who was an opponent of General Manuel Avila Camacho. My vote didn't make a difference as General Avila Camacho became president.

Bullfights were very popular in Nogales, Mexico. When I heard that the famous bullfighter Lorenzo Garza, known as El Magnifico, was coming to town, I decided to go and get a glimpse of him as he arrived. I saw him arrive at the bullring, and was so excited that I wanted to see him fight the bulls. I didn't have any money to pay for a ticket, so I ran to a nearby hill where one could see part of the bullring. After watching whatever I could of him fighting the bulls, I decided that I would like to be a bullfighter. I even posed like a bullfighter whenever anyone took a picture of me.

Mexican Youth Legion Member - Albino

Brother-in-law - Pedro and sister Dolores Zavala

Chapter IX

A MORE LUCRATIVE
SOURCE OF INCOME

One of the most well-known sources of income in Nogales, Mexico, was the passing of contraband into Mexico. During the forties, silk was very much in demand in Mexico City and other cities to the south—women's stockings and underwear, in particular. Also in demand were dresses and cosmetics, which were not allowed across the border without payment of duty fees. The profit on these goods was obviously greater if one was able to bring the merchandise into Mexico without paying the duty fees. People were able to avoid the duties if they wore the new dress or garment across the border. There were many people who earned a living wearing merchandise across the border into Mexico. A woman could wear a new dress across the border for somebody else for a small fee, and could make several trips in the course of a day. From time to time, I would see my mother wearing a new dress as she crossed the border, and I knew she was trying to earn a few coins. Most of the garments taken across the border were for *fayuqueros*—these were men and women who would take the merchandise and sell it further south of the border. Merchants in Nogales, Arizona, knew that women's silk underwear and stockings that were bought in big quantities had to be wrapped in small packages so fayuqueros could hide them under their coats or blouses as they crossed the border.

Pullman crews got wind of high profits to be made transporting contraband goods that were in big demand in large cities like Guadalajara and Mexico City. They began to buy large quantities of goods, and would ask my nephew and me to find ways of crossing the merchandise into Mexico without paying duties. We started transporting the contraband by tying packages around our waists and around our ankles while wearing loose coats and wide-legged pants. Once a week, we would make as much as thirty-six pesos, which was the equivalent of three dollars. In those days, it was fairly good money for us. We made our living that way for about a year. Since I was buying clothing to be transported across the border, I became very familiar with most of the stores in Nogales, Arizona. The Ville De Paris was the biggest, followed by the El Paso Clothing Store. It was at this last store that I began eyeing the men's suits. The day finally came when I was able to buy my first suit with fifteen dollars I had saved. It was a navy blue striped suit. I remember the first time I put it on. People who knew me couldn't believe what they were seeing. That night, I went to the plaza and stood there while a kid shined my shoes. Girls stared at me, perhaps more because I was a novelty to them than anything else. But to me, it was a dream come true. A new suit! Wow!

There was a short girl who always walked the plaza in the evening with friends. She always smiled at me. One Saturday night, I waited for her to come by. Finally, she and her girlfriends walked by, and she called out to me, "Adios!" which was a common greeting as you passed by. That evening, a friend and I began following the girls. We finally made contact, and were able to befriend two of the girls. From then on, we both had girlfriends and our girlfriends were cousins.

We started going to dances with them much to my concern because I had never danced on a dance floor before. However, in time, I became a smooth foot dragger. I used to admire dancers who could jitterbug. The best music I could sort of shuffle to was Glenn Miller's "In the Mood." which I enjoyed doing. I went out with my new girlfriend for about three months and then, for some reason, dropped her. She never forgave me for doing that. My friend Agustin, whom we called Tilin, eventually married the other girl.

I continued passing contraband for a living until one night, my nephew Johnny, one another kid—I can't remember who he was—and I had three gunnysacks of merchandise that included silks and cosmetics. We decided to wait until dark so we could cross unobserved. We then crossed the fence in the dark through a canyon near where we lived and headed toward our house, which was one of the first houses in the outskirts of the neighborhood. We were walking among cactus plants when all of a sudden, out of nowhere, a customs agent appeared right in front of us. With his flashlight, he inspected our bags and told us that we were under arrest. He then walked us up and down the hills to the custom house by the railroad yard where we were placed under arrest. We spent the night in a room with a guard at the door. Two days later, we were turned over to the police department, and were imprisoned for about two weeks. After appearing before a judge, we were set free because we were juveniles.

Prior to that incident, if we had a lot of goods to transport, we would bring them to trains that were ready to leave the next day. The customs building was right next to the railroad yard, so we would sneak the goods aboard the Pullman cars at night while no one was around. We had a key to the Pullman cars, and would board in the dark. Each Pullman car had a large dressing room with a lavatory, a toilet, and a shower. The lavatories had a couple of light fixtures, which we removed with a screwdriver. We would tie the flat packages to one another with a string and drop them in between the hollow walls and then we would replace the fixtures. When the train was inspected by the customs inspectors before passengers boarded, they never imagined that there was contraband hanging in between the walls of the Pullman cars. After we got caught with contraband on that dark night, I decided that I needed to do something else for a living. That's when I decided to leave home for good and venture on to new horizons.

The first place I chose to go was to the place of my birth, Phoenix, Arizona. There, I could look for my sister Josefa and perhaps find a job. I wasn't used to being away from home although on one occasion, a friend of mine, who worked as a radio technician for a Philco Radio Dealer, invited me to go with him on a promotional tour to towns in northern Mexico like Imuris, Magdalena, Altar, Pitiquito, and Caborca. He had a record player in his old car with speakers mounted on top. We would stop at ranches that were in the middle of nowhere. We would look for an empty lot where we could organize a dance, play music from the car and advertise radios at the same time. We would ask people if they wanted to dedicate a song to someone—using our microphone. That was my first experience being away from home beyond overnight. I found it very exciting driving through dusty, bumpy roads to towns I didn't know existed.

The day finally arrived when I was to leave the town where I had spent a good part of my childhood and teenage life—a town where I lived in misery not knowing where my next meal would come from; a town where I learned to see, hear, touch, smell, and taste what poverty was all about. I was leaving behind my mother, brothers Tony and Isidro, my nephews Johnny and Amador, and my niece Dora who grew up with us. I was also leaving behind my close friends Agustin (Tilin), El Chapito, Juan Hernandez "El Negrito," El Capullo, and others whom I would never see again. Adios, amigos!

Brother - Antonio and Nephew - Johnny T. Chavez

Brother - Antonio, Friend - Ricardo Obregon, Albino

Chapter X

MY MOVE TO PHOENIX

The day came when I felt old enough to venture on my own so I decided to return to the city of my birth, Phoenix, Arizona. I hadn't the slightest idea what I was going to do or where I was going to live. After eight years across the border, I had forgotten how to speak English. All I knew was that once in Phoenix, I was going to look for my half sister Josefa who lived somewhere in the area. I took the Greyhound bus from Nogales, Arizona, to Phoenix; and I don't recall much about the trip. All I remember is that it was early in the year, around February 1942, that I arrived in the evening and that all I had with me was a small suitcase and five dollars in my pocket. I got off the bus, and noticed several hotels across the street. The bus station was near skid row. The hotels nearby serviced hobos and skid row types. I saw a hotel about a couple of blocks from the bus station, and as I walked toward the hotel, a drunk came up to me and asked if he could help me with my suitcase. At that moment, a police officer was driving by and stopped. The policeman came over and asked if the guy was bothering me, and I said no. The officer left and the drunk also left in a hurry.

I arrived at a hotel that was renting rooms for a dollar a night. I went in and don't recall how I made myself understood by the hotel clerk, but I was able to rent a room for two nights for a total of two dollars. When I walked into my room, I was surprised to find a double bed, a cabinet with a washbowl, and towels. Seeing all those luxury items, I didn't know how to react. I had never slept in a double bed all by myself. Staying at a hotel was a new experience for me as well. At the time, I wouldn't have known the difference between a Hilton and a Motel 6. After paying for the room, all I had left was three dollars. The next morning, I got up really early and went across the street to a small restaurant called Greasy Joe's. I went in and the customers were nothing but hobos and winos. But for a person with my resources, it was an okay place since a bowl of chili beans cost five cents, and a hamburger cost ten cents. After breakfast, I went to a nearby street corner where a group of men were standing waiting for farm contractors to come and pick up workers. I joined them, and was lucky that I got picked up to work in a lettuce field. I worked all day stacking lettuce boxes on the trucks that went around the field picking up full boxes of lettuce. The great mistake I made that day was not taking a lunch with me and when lunchtime came, I was hungry. Seeing all the other workers eating their lunches was torture for me. Mexican workers had their tacos and the hobos had their boloney. The hobos ate sliced boloney with crackers. I couldn't stand it and no one bothered to ask me if I wanted to share some of their food. I remember walking behind the truck and eating lettuce hearts until I was full. All that afternoon, I kept thinking of a bowl of chili beans. I ended up making three dollars that day which was a pretty good wage for me. As soon as they brought us back into town, I was starving so I immediately hit Greasy Joe's.

The following day, I was also picked up, but it turned out that the job was doing *desaije* (thinning lettuce sprouts). A short-handled hoe was given to each worker to thin out the lettuce sprouts so that each sprout would be six inches apart. That meant bending down all day long. Aside from my previous day's work, this was my first experience working in a field. Each worker took a row and started hoeing. Fifteen minutes later, I noticed that the rest of the workers were about a quarter of a mile ahead of me. I had only advanced about twenty feet and was struggling to leave one sprout every six inches. When the foreman saw me trying my best and yet not advancing, he came over and tried to show me how to do the work quickly, but it didn't work. Fifteen minutes later, he came and told me that I just wasn't cutting it, so he took the hoe away from me and let me go. Since we were many miles away from town, I had to sit by the truck for the rest of the day until it was time for the others to go home. It ended up being another long day for me, and worst of all, with no pay.

The day I worked in the lettuce field, I thought that it would be a steady job for a while. I didn't realize that farm work was not steady. I stayed at the same hotel, but didn't get picked up for work the next day. So, I moved to another hotel nearby called the Tourister, which was on Madison Avenue. Rooms rented for seventy-five cents a night. I also learned that there was an open porch upstairs that had a bunch of army cots with a blanket that rented for only twenty-five cents a night. A couple of days went by, and I couldn't find work. I met a blonde Mexican guy who was staying at that same hotel, and he was in the same situation I was in. He told me his life story and how he had been in prison several times. He told me that he had a friend who lived in Phoenix and that perhaps his friend could tell us where to find a job. We went to see the fellow and as they were talking, the friend lit a homemade cigarette that had a strange smell. Both guys then began to smoke the cigarette. I had heard of marijuana, but did not know anything about it. Later on, I learned that they had been smoking marijuana. To this day, I am grateful that they did not offer me a puff. At the time, I was just a naive seventeen-year-old kid. That night, the friend invited us to the house of a woman he was living with who turned out to be a really nice person. She asked us to stay for dinner, which was most appreciated. After that, I lost touch with my new acquaintance, perhaps for the best—he might have been a bad influence on me.

I met another Mexican guy in the hotel who suggested that we go to Montana because they needed sheepherders. I wasn't experienced enough to jump on a train and head for unknown places like Montana. A few nights later, I was on my last quarter, when my nephew Johnny showed up. He was younger than I, and also had come looking for work. That night, I could only rent one cot with my last quarter, and Johnny didn't have a place to stay, so we strategized and decided that I should rent a cot. After dark, I waited for all the hobos to go to sleep and then signaled to Johnny. He then climbed up the porch by holding onto the roof drains. I told him he had to hide his head under the blanket when we slept because the night clerk came several times during the night to make sure that the drunks were not causing disturbances. The night clerk always carried a club just in case. Fortunately, we made it through the night without getting caught.

The next morning, we were picked up to go to a cotton field far from downtown Phoenix. We picked cotton under the hot summer sun, and by noon, our hands were a bloody mess from scratches. At noon, we weighed the cotton we had picked all morning, and got paid. We made enough money to buy a couple of donuts and a pint of milk. On the way back that evening, I remember that there was an accident on the road in the middle of nowhere. A pickup truck had turned over with two men riding in the back—it looked like one had gotten thrown out of the truck, and the other had hung on. When the truck turned upside down, one of the arms of the guy who had held on was severed; the other man was unconscious, moaning now and then. To me, it was one of the most helpless experiences I had ever had. A man was holding on to the stub of the man's arm to slow the bleeding while others were taking care of the other injured man. We left and never knew what happened after that.

The following day, Johnny and I went looking for my step-sister Josefa. I don't recall how, but we found out where she was living. So we took the local bus, which went to the outskirts of Phoenix, and then walked the rest of the way to the ranch where she lived. When we got to the door of her house, she was making tortillas, and had a ball of dough in her hand. When she saw us, she threw the dough to the floor and rushed to embrace us. We hadn't seen each other since 1933 when I left for Mexico. We visited for a while and then Johnny left for Nogales. I stayed with my step-sister for a couple of weeks. Then, my other half sister Dolores sent me a bus ticket to come to California, so I left for Santa Paula, California.

Albino

Chapter XI

MOVE TO CALIFORNIA

It was sometime in late March of 1942 when I left for Santa Paula. It was the longest trip I had ever taken. I don't remember anything about the trip on the Greyhound bus. I do remember walking out the front door of the bus terminal in downtown Los Angeles and feeling like I had arrived in another world with all the jukeboxes playing Glenn Miller music. It was really early in the morning and as I stood outside the terminal, I was in awe of all the tall buildings and the noise of streetcars going by and newspaper boys yelling, "Read all about it!" With the war going on, there were soldiers and sailors everywhere.

Later in the morning, I took the next bus for Santa Paula. As we passed through Burbank, I could see war planes taking off from what I later learned was the Lockheed Plant and Airport. There was a lot of excitement everywhere. I kept thinking to myself, *Where will I be when I reach the age of eighteen?* As I was just a youth in my late teens, I could see a life full of opportunity in front of me. I was so excited about those potential opportunities. But with the war going on, I thought to myself, *What does the future hold for me?*

As we approached Santa Paula, I was straining to peek ahead through the bus window. I could see many trees, but couldn't see the skyscrapers that I thought existed in Santa Paula. The bus depot was on Eighth Street, just south of the main street. When I got off the bus, I saw this woman walking toward me with a smile on her face, and I immediately knew that she was my step-sister Lola.

We hugged, and as she drove me to her home, I kept looking at the mountains so near to town. I found Santa Paula a very beautiful and exciting town. I met my nephews and my niece, and they made me feel at home. So did my step-sister and my brother-in-law Pete. Their home at the time was a small wooden-framed house with three small bedrooms located at the corner of Santa Paula and Sycamore streets. Across Santa Paula Street was a baseball field where the locals played baseball.

Shortly after my arrival, I went to pick lemons for a couple of days. The number of scratches on my hands and arms outnumbered the lemons I picked. I don't recall what happened in the weeks that followed, but I do remember that as soon as school was out, we all headed up north to follow the crops. Our first stop was Morro Bay. We got hired to pick peas. Part of my job was spraying the plants with DDT from a tank I carried on my back. The tank had a hand pump with a hose that I used to spray the plants. Now that I look back, I don't recall anybody telling me to wear gloves or a mask. There was an abandoned farmhouse across the road from the field, which is where we set up camp. Part of my family stayed in the house, and the rest stayed in a tent. The house was also being used by some of the other workers. It was there that I met other Santa Paulans. I met a very short old man whom we called Don Chanito. He stands out in my mind because he was missing some front teeth and always greeted people with a grin. What was funny about him was that as he picked peas, he was always chewing on one. In fact, his mouth was always green from chewing on peas. Here, I was spraying DDT on the plants ahead of those harvesting, and he was eating the peas without washing them. The other thing that stands out in my mind is the morning when we discovered a cow that had died during the night. Someone suggested that since the cow had just died, the meat was okay to eat. I remember seeing several persons cutting big chunks of meat off the dead cow. I stuck to frijoles.

One evening after work, my nephew Freddie and I walked to a store in nearby Morro Bay. On the way back, a sailor picked us up and gave us a ride in his car. The narrow road was nothing but curves, and the sailor was taking those curves at high speed. I was scared to death. I wasn't used to riding in cars. When he dropped us off, I remember heaving a deep sigh of relief.

From Morro Bay, we moved onto a farm near the small town of Oceano, California. We occupied a farmhouse that was empty, and as I look back now, I believe those empty farmhouses belonged to Japanese families who had been taken to internment camps. Our stay on that farm was very short because the only work available in the area was irrigating a sugar beet field, and only my brother-in-law Pete had gotten a job. One funny experience stands out from my brief stay there. One day, Pete bought a half gallon of sweet raisin wine and left it on the porch of the house. Freddie and I decided that he had forgotten about it, so we began to drink it. It was really sweet, and the more we drank, the better it tasted. After a while, we began to feel a little high; so we decided to walk over to the town of Oceano, which was just a store and a couple of other buildings away. Since no one ever questioned my age, given my height, I went in to a store and bought a couple of beers. We drank them as we walked along the road. The next thing I remember was waking up before sundown in a cemetery near Arroyo Grande. We found out that mixing wine and beer can knock you out. I imagine Pete must have wondered what happened to his half gallon of raisin wine.

From Oceano, we moved on to Mission San Jose where we ended up at a farm owned by a Portuguese man named Manuel and his young son. They lived in a huge red barn but didn't occupy the entire barn. So they let us live in the unoccupied part. We only worked a very short time for them.

I also remember working for a man who grew tomatoes near Livermore, California. I would ride with him every day over the mountains through a road full of curves. One morning, on our way to work, a car that was behind us tried to pass us on a blind curve. It infuriated the man so he decided he wasn't going to let the other driver pass us. Every time the other driver tried to pass us, the man would speed up, terrifying me in the process. I kept imagining us going down an embankment. We finally made it to the bottom of the hill and onto a straight road. The other driver finally passed us.

My job with the man from Livermore was riding on a contraption that was pulled by a small tractor. In the contraption, there was a water tank and a box with tomato plants next to me. I would push a pedal, and water would squirt from the water tank onto the ground. I would then stick a tomato plant in the wet ground at the same time. I made fifty cents an hour. The job didn't last very long. I also remember getting another job picking apricots with the rest of the family.

It was in Mission San Jose that I first met Margaret, Lupe, and Tony Vasquez from Santa Paula. They were working somewhere nearby. Margaret later married my brother Tony.

After I left Mission San Jose, I got a job working at a cannery in nearby Centerville, California. I made 60 cents an hour and later on, got a 3 cent raise. While I was working at the cannery, I received a notice to register for induction into the army. I had turned eighteen and Uncle Sam wanted me.

I bought my first automobile for forty dollars while working at the cannery. It was an old Model A convertible with a rumble seat. I bought the Model A even though I didn't have a driver's license. I drove it for about a week and then the tires began to come apart. I was also putting more oil in the engine than I could afford, so I took it back and told the dealer he could have his car back.

After the fruit season, we moved back to Santa Paula where I joined the Laborers' Union and went to work nights at the Port Hueneme Base. At the time, they were building cylindrical structures cut in half called Quonset huts to house navy personnel. A railroad spur was also being constructed to carry materials into the base. I worked with the crews that were installing the railroad tracks until January 1943. In January, I was called in for induction into the army and was taken with a bunch of other guys to Fresno, California, where we took our physical. I passed and was declared fit for duty. I was told that I would be called soon. Shortly after, I left Fresno and returned to Santa Paula.

One day, I went to a grocery store on the main street called El Brillante. As I went in, I noticed three or four girls behind the counter. I assumed they were sisters. There was one in particular who attracted my attention. I thought she was very pretty. Nonetheless, I bought whatever I had gone in to buy and walked away without giving the girl any more thought. It so happened that sometime later, my nephew Freddie and I went to the movies, and lo and behold, sitting in front of us were the girls from the store! My nephew who knew them began to talk to them, and pretty soon, they asked us to sit with them. I sat next to the one I had my eye on. We talked mostly in Spanish because she probably detected that my English wasn't very good. After the show, we agreed to a movie date. I think it was a week later that we met by the theater. She was wearing a powder blue suit and her oldest brother, Johnny, was with her. We went into the theater and in the course of the show, I got a kiss from her. Fortunately, her brother had agreed to sit a few rows away from us. After that, we met several times. She was attending a beauty school in Los Angeles and invited me to go see her in Los Angeles. I took her up on her offer and went to visit her. We went to see a program at the Million Dollar Theatre and from there, we went to an all-night show where we spent most of the night watching movies.

Naomi came from a large family. She had a step-brother Tino Martinez, five brothers-Johnnie, Sam, Victor, David and Robert and four sisters-Toni, Stella, Alice and Lydia. Tita Vargas, a cousin from Mexico, also lived with Naomi's family.

Soon after meeting Naomi, I volunteered to go with the next group of inductees instead of waiting to be called. The next thing I remember is saying goodbye to my sweetheart Naomi as I boarded the bus that was to take my group to the induction center in Monterey, California for processing into the United States Armed Forces.

Brothers - Antonio, Manuel, Ysidro
Mother - Dolores and Niece - Dora T. Chavez

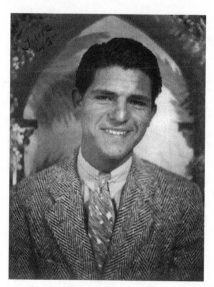

Albino R. Pineda

The Salas Family: Back Row: Johnnie, Naomi, Tino, mother with Lydia in arms, Father Juan, Estella, Toni, Front Row: Sam Alice and Victor

Chapter XII

MY SERVICE IN THE U.S. ARMY

After our arrival at the induction center, my group and others were processed. We were given vaccination shots and a crew-cut haircut. The next day, we started training on how to march in cadence. That turned out to be a comedy of errors. When a "Rear march!" order was given, some of the recruits would turn about while others kept going forward, bumping into one another. It took a couple of days, after a cadre of corporals yelled their guts out, to get the group to march in order. Every morning before breakfast, we would stand in line for roll call. The instructors would start by yelling out our names and we would respond, "Here!" When they got to my name, they would call out, "Pindah! Pindah!" When there was no response, they would spell the name out, "P-I-N-E-D-A!" Then, I would reply, "Here!" Then, the corporal who acted like a general would yell back, "Wake up, soldier!" I discovered that they were guys from the East Coast who had never dealt with Spanish names. Martinez was "Martineeze," Lopez was "Lopeeze," and I was "Pindah." I ended up with the name Pineedah the rest of my army days.

Next, we were issued uniforms and a pair of big shoes with leggings. Recruits were pushed around something awful. Once we got all our shots, uniforms, and basic training, we were loaded on a train and shipped to different training camps around the country. I ended up at Camp Swift, Texas, which was about sixty miles east of Austin. I was assigned to an artillery battalion. After my arrival, my main concern was that I couldn't speak English very well. Fortunately, I discovered that in my battalion, there were about nine

Mexican-Americans from Santa Paula; and others from San Jose, Porterville, and other parts of California. In fact, many of the other soldiers were from the West Coast. Of the nine Mexican-Americans from Santa Paula, five were in my same battery. That made me feel good because I was with a group with whom I could communicate in Spanish. What I found to be funny was that most of these guys came from a zoot suit or pachuco background, and they thought that I considered myself better than them because I couldn't speak their pachuco lingo. I had never been around pachucos, so I was ignorant of their culture. However, we all got along very well. They would laugh at my English pronunciations since I couldn't roll my *r*'s in words like "iron," "Charles," and "curious," to name a few.

We started our basic training with the Ml rifles, and later, we started to train as an artillery battalion using the 105 mm Howitzer. I was assigned to Battery B of the 261st Field Artillery Battalion. I liked marching, and soon, I was assigned to carry the battery's guidon flag. I would march at the head of the unit on hikes and parade reviews. Because of my interest in the army, I was asked if I wanted to be in charge of logistics for our battery, but I declined due to my poor English. I believe that if I had been proficient in the English language, I would have applied for Officer Candidate School. I would have made a good army officer because I liked the army at the time. Every time we went on a fifteen-mile hike with full gear on our backs, I, as the battery emblem carrier, was supposed to end the hike at the front of the column, which I did, while many others would drop out or not arrive until hours later.

In the field, we all became proficient at digging foxholes. I had never dug so many holes in the ground before. Part of our training was to go out on a two or three day bivouac, and place our cannon at a previously selected site. Small red flags would indicate where to set up our two-man pup tents. I had always been deathly afraid of snakes of any kind. On one of these occasions, the red flag for my tent was on top of a pile of dead oak branches. When my partner and I started to clear the branches, a green snake bolted from the pile of branches to the limb of a nearby oak tree. I froze because I had never seen a snake jump from the ground to a tree. I was shook up, but continued to clear the spot. In my mind, I kept thinking, *Sure enough, when I go to bed, there are going to be snakes in our tent.* Just in case, when I got into my sleeping bag that night, I zipped it from head to toe.

During my army days, I weighed 133 lbs. And even though I ate everything I could get my hands on, I never gained any weight. After lunch, I would rush to the PX if I had any money and would down a pint of ice cream.

On certain weekends, we would get a weekend pass to Austin. While in Austin, we would rent rooms from private families, which was very common for soldiers on weekend pass. I remember one time I took a taxi to go to the Mexican barrio where all the bars were. When the taxi came to an intersection, we hit another car, or we got hit and the taxi rolled over. I crawled out and not wanting to get involved with the law, made myself scarce. The family from whom I rented a room had a jukebox, and early in the morning, they played Glenn Miller music. It was always fun for me as a young soldier to go on a weekend pass and "do the town" as we used to say.

The army did things in odd but, I suppose, practical ways. Every time we were due for a physical, they would make all of us take all our clothes off and put on a raincoat. They would pack us up like cattle in a truck and take us to the infirmary for the physical. So every time we saw a truck full of GIs wearing raincoats on a sunny day, we knew where they were going. However, in Texas, it wasn't unusual to carry a raincoat on a sunny day because when one least expected it, a big cloud might come by and create a sudden downpour.

Digging foxholes in the hot Texas sun made us sweat by the bucketful. The army fatigues we wore in the field were always white around the collar and along the back from the salt we "sweated out." Salt pills were part of our daily intake.

It was at Camp Swift that I saw a contingent of African Corps prisoners of war being escorted into a special prisoner's area. They were a proud bunch. They wore black uniforms with the long-billed caps and riveted boots, which made a distinctive sound.

While in basic training, I would see things that were funny to me. I remember one of our guys getting into some kind of trouble and his being confined to the barracks. If he wanted to go to the PX, he had to go with another soldier carrying a rifle to guard him. One night, he was escorted to the PX and when they got there, the guard told the prisoner, who was one of his buddies, to hold the rifle while he went in and bought some beer.

After basic training, we were loaded onto trucks with all our belongings (duffel bag and rifle); and were taken on a convoy to Camp Bowie, Texas, where we spent the night. From there, we continued on to Fort Sill, Oklahoma, where we were to spend over a year training with new artillery officers. When we first arrived, we were housed in large tents; then we were taken to our permanent quarters, which turned out to be large multi-floor buildings. The buildings were beautiful with spacious lawns for assemblies and review parades. Inside the buildings, the floors were shiny like a mirror and there were large showers for bathing, a cafeteria, and a large dayroom for games. Behind the buildings was a paved street, and across the street a series of buildings to house our cannons and trucks. Fort Sill was a regular army installation with a PX, a movie theater, and a museum which showed where the great Indian chief Geronimo had been held captive. And nearby, was the town of Lawton, Oklahoma, where we could go and have a good time.

It was at Fort Sill that I went through some unforgettable experiences. As a private, I was paid thirty dollars a month. I would send twenty of the thirty dollars to my mother as she was my dependant. This resulted in my always being short of money. I wanted to go to town and have a few beers, like the rest of the men, but being broke kept me in camp on weekends. So, to earn a few extra dollars, I began to pull guard duty for others on weekends. I would charge three dollars for four hours. I recall enduring some really cold nights during the winter doing this work. Also, for some reason or another, the army never fed me enough food. I was always hungry, and being broke didn't help.

I remember vividly that one night we went on an overnight bivouac. Our cannon was placed right next to a frozen creek, and some of us in the gun crew covered ourselves with a big heavy canvas to ward off the chill of the night. The following day before lunch, one of our crew members, whom we considered to be an old man because he was twenty-four years old, began to carefully unwrap a Twinkie right next to me. I thought he was going to offer me a piece, but instead, he began to savor every morsel with gusto. It was at that point that I realized how the army had begun to change us. There was a time when smokers would offer a cigarette to the person next to them before lighting up for themselves. This was no longer the case. Each individual was out for himself. Sometimes, at camp, if you were at the wrong end of the table during chow time, chances were that you would not get your fair share of the food. The only times I gorged myself with food was on holidays or when I served as KP in the kitchen.

As I have mentioned before, it was at Fort Sill that I experienced some times I will never forget. The first experience came when I read that the army needed paratroopers for the expected invasion of Europe. The army was paying fifty dollars a month for a paratrooper at the private level. I thought that an additional twenty dollars a month was just what I needed. I filed an application for a transfer, and when it got to my battalion commander, he sent word that he wanted me to report to him. I went to his office and stood at attention before his desk. He said, "At ease!" I was so tense that I just remained at attention. He then asked why I was asking to transfer to a parachute outfit. In my broken English, I tried to convey to him that some of the guys were always making fun of my English, which wasn't really true. I didn't want to tell him that I needed more money. In response, he said, "Do you realize that you are not fit to be a paratrooper? Paratroopers are tough guys that come from the alleys where they're used to fighting all the time. They are rough men ready for anything." And he continued, "As I have looked at your records, you don't come from that kind of background. I think you will do all right where you're at. Besides, let me advise you. If anyone makes fun of your English, kick them where it hurts, and I will support you." I saluted him and left his office with a feeling I had never had before. Nobody in my life had ever given me that kind of caring and supportive advice. After the invasion at Normandy, I realized that had I gone into the paratroopers, I would probably have ended like many of them—dead. Through the years, I have always treasured that advice.

During this period of time, my girlfriend Naomi wrote to me almost three times a week. I waited for her letters like I did for food. She was my future. To this day, I have all of her letters, most of which were in Spanish.

Another important experience that changed my life occurred when I decided to enroll in an English correspondence course. This occurred while I was still at Fort Sill. Once I began the course, I fell in love with the English language. I would study every lesson until the lights went out at night. That course gave me a new outlook on life. The study of Abraham Lincoln's life thrilled me. Then came a series of classics in a nutshell version such as *Vanity Fair* and "Rip Van Winkle." I read Scott Fitzgerald's works and poems by Robert Burns, Henry Wadsworth Longfellow, and others with great appreciation and enthusiasm. I bought a thick Spanish-English dictionary, which was one of the best investments I had ever made. I would listen to the radio, pick up words that I didn't know, and rush to my dictionary to find their meanings. I wanted to learn new words and especially proper pronunciation. I still have that dictionary and the lessons I received from the correspondence course as treasured mementos. After a few months of study, I was able to speak and write enough English to understand others and make myself understood. I remember reading my first novel ever, *The Razor's Edge* by W. S. Maugham. Later on, I saw the movie with Tyrone Power. From then on, my duffel bag was full of books. I loved to read then, and still do today. I used to go to Lawton's USO where they had a small library. Once, I found an old English grammar book, which had all the parts of speech; and in the final pages, it had some poems such as "The Light Brigade," "The Tree," and several others that caught my interest. I borrowed the book and got so engrossed in it that I never returned it. That was one dishonest thing I did while in the service. I still have that book.

While at Fort Sill, we were subjected to listening to lectures by a captain who supposedly knew all about different cultures and countries. I still remember a couple of his lectures. The first one was about China. He said that Chinese people were lazy, dirty, and inferior to other races. There was at least one Chinese soldier in the audience, and I felt sorry for him. Another lecture that he presented still reverberates in my mind, and that was on Mexico. He said that Mexicans were dirty, lazy, and had no sense of morality. The lecturer didn't care that there were a number of soldiers of Mexican descent in the audience. A soldier was the property of the U.S. Army, a GI issue with no right to speak. You were there to listen. I doubt whether those things are said or tolerated in today's army.

During my stay at Fort Sill, I was able to get a long furlough. I remember boarding a Greyhound bus on my way to the West Coast. I remember sitting next to an Anglo girl from Texas about my age on her way to Amarillo. In the front seat was her little brother who must have been around eight years old. There was a change of bus in Fort Worth; and I was able to go to the USO and take a shower, which I ended up regretting as I will discuss in a moment. The girl and I shared adjacent seats as we continued on to Amarillo. We became so chummy that I ended up kissing her with her young brother staring from the front seat. She got off in Amarillo, and I went on to Tucson, Arizona, to see my mother and brothers in nearby Nogales, Mexico. I got off the bus and began to hitchhike to Nogales, Arizona. A car stopped, and the driver offered me ride. The occupants of the car turned out to be an army captain and his wife on their way to Nogales. They were going just to visit. He asked me where I was from and other questions about Nogales, Mexico. It was a welcome and pleasant ride.

The day after I arrived in Nogales, I discovered that I had contracted a bad case of athlete's foot, which also covered my hands. I got it when I took the shower at the USO in Forth Worth, Texas. In time, I was able to get rid of the infection on my hands but not on my feet. To prevent a flare-up, I had to dry my feet well after showering and use a medicated powder.

In Nogales, I stayed a few days with my mother who lived only a little better than when I left home. My army allowance helped a great deal as my two younger brothers still lived with her. After a few days in Nogales, I left for California to visit my sister and, of course, my girlfriend who was expecting me. When I got to Santa Paula, my girlfriend took me to meet her father, whom I had met before in a barbershop. He asked me if I was related to the Zavalas who were customers at his grocery store. I also remember taking Naomi out on a date the next day. The following day, she told me that her father wanted to talk to me again. I somehow felt that he wanted to scold me for not asking for his permission to take his daughter out. The following day, I went to their house and sat on the sofa. When he came in, he greeted me and sat down next to me. He told me it was common decency for a young man like me to ask for permission before taking someone's daughter out on a date. He was very stern about it, and as I sat there listening to him, I kept rubbing my hands. Finally, I apologized for my actions. Naomi, meanwhile, had disappeared from the scene. After that, I was invited to have lunch.

After my furlough was over, I returned to Fort Sill and continued with my English lessons. Later, as D-day approached, our battalion was shipped to Fort Polk, Louisiana. There we were trained on how to use the large 155 mm Long Tom cannons. It took a crew of fifteen men to man those guns. My position on those guns was to raise the gun for distance and to pull the firing lanyard. It took four men to load the shells. While in Louisiana, I became even more aware of my difficulty in rolling the *r*'s in my English conversations. There was a town nearby where some of the men went called Lake Charles in Louisiana. For the life of me, I could not properly pronounce the word "Charles." My tongue just couldn't roll the *r* properly. I had the same trouble with the words "iron" and "curious." It took a long time before I could overcome that problem. While at Camp Polk, I remember going on a one-night pass to a nearby town and gorging on hot dogs and beer. Those were fun nights.

Sergeant - Manuel R. Pineda
(Elpidio began to use Manuel as his name)

Camp Polk Lousiana - 155 mm Cannon

Naomi M. Salas, Albino R. Pineda, Toni M. Salas

Albino R. Pineda

Albino R. Pineda

Privates - John Romero and Albino R. Pineda

Privates - John Romero, Silvero Mendez, Albino R. Pineda

Albino Pineda and Naomi Salas

My Girlfriend - Naomi Salas

Private - Albino R. Pineda, on furlough

Chapter XIII

BOUND FOR OVERSEAS

By September 20, 1944, our cannons were polished, cosmolined and ready to go. On that day, we boarded a train made up of Pullman cars en route to a staging area at Camp Miles Standish, Taunton, Massachusetts. At night, we shared bunks in the train. In our outfit, there was a young heavy-set black Portuguese fellow. Nobody could understand why he was in a white unit. In fact, when we were in Texas during our basic training, he would go with us to town, but was not allowed in the restaurants with us. On our way to Boston on the train, nobody wanted to share bunks with him. We used to call him Boogie-woogie because he was always shaking his body in a dance. He ended up sharing a bunk with me all the way to Massachusetts. To me, he wasn't any different from the rest of the men.

The train ride was an exciting experience, especially going across the south and up through the northeastern states. When the train stopped briefly in Lima, Ohio, I went out to the vestibule, opened the door, and all I could see were railroad cars. Suddenly, a young girl came and sat on the steps of the Pullman and began to talk to me. As the train began to move and pick up speed, she hung on talking to me. Finally, she said goodbye and jumped off the fast-moving train. We kept waving to each other until she disappeared from sight. The train took us right to Camp Miles Standish where our battalion was processed and received a last-minute security lecture. We then went to board the USS *West Point*, once known as *Luxury Liner America*. It no longer looked like a luxury liner, but then, we were not passengers going on a pleasure trip.

The ship was waiting for us and for many other troops from all over the United States that were also boarding that day. As we arrived at the docks with our duffel bags, our last names were called, and we would respond with our first name and middle initial and board the ship. October 3 and 4 were the days for boarding with October 4 the day of sailing. Just to reaffirm that this was not a pleasure cruise, the 261st Artillery Battalion was assigned the duties of security guard and kitchen details aboard the ship. My guard duty was to let light came on which meant they had to put their cigarettes out and go back to their quarters. I still don't know how I was able to tolerate a hallway full of smoke and the smell of many bodies.

When we sailed on the 4th in the late afternoon, I was on duty and didn't realize that the ship, which was carrying fifteen thousand troops, was moving away from port. When I finally came out on the main deck for fresh air, to my surprise, all I could see was the Boston skyline in the far distance. At that moment, a sense of sadness came over me, and I thought, *Will I ever see this land again?* Our ship was a fast-moving ship and had no escorts. It zigzagged for nine days until we got to Liverpool, England. Midway across the ocean, we met the *Queen Mary*, which was a troop transport at the time, heading for the United States. During our voyage, I, along with many other soldiers, was seasick all the way. The mere smell of the inside of the ship made me sick. The ship's dining room had tables that were very high with no chairs. One had to eat standing up. The smell of the ship, coupled with the smell of greasy fried potatoes, caused many of the men to throw up while having breakfast. We endured nine days of stomach-renching experiences, not to mention the fear of a U-boat torpedoing our ship. Eventually, we anchored in the bay of Liverpool, England, where we spent the night. The next day, in the late morning, the ship lifted anchor and slowly moved toward the dock. As we docked, there were English longshoremen down below on the docks looking up at the troops aboard the ship. Soldiers would throw candy bars down at them, and they would all run for them. We remained on board the ship for the rest of the afternoon, and in the evening, we started to disembark and walk across the docks to a waiting train. My duffel bag was heavier than most because half of its contents were books. We rode the train south, and at every stop, there were USO women waiting with big pots of tea and donuts for the troops.

Our initial stop was in a small town called Milton but eventually out battalion was spread throughout several villages. Our particular battery was housed several yards from the English Channel. The place was known as Barton on the Sea. At one time, the area had been a vacationer's favorite. We shared an old hotel with some British soldiers. Our bunks had straw mats instead of mattresses and the lighting consisted of little pipes sticking out from the walls, which could be lit with a match once the gas was turned on. The lighting was very old-fashioned lighting. Our cannons, which were attached to the mechanical tractors, were parked along the street. From our cannons, we could see the Isle of Wight to the east. From time to time, we could see long convoys of ships heading across the channel. We arrived at Barton on the Sea on October 13, 1944, and stayed there for about two months. During that time, we rarely saw the sun. It was always windy and drizzly.

One night, I was on guard duty in the street and it was drizzling, windy, and dark. All of a sudden, out of the darkness, a bobby appeared in his dark uniform and scared "the dickens out of me." He started to talk to me with his English accent, and I couldn't understand a word he was saying. I would just say, "Yes, ahuh!" and nod my head. Finally, he left into the darkness, probably wondering what was wrong with me. In time, I began to understand the English a little better, especially the women I met at pubs in the evenings. I would walk a mile or two in the pitch darkness of the night looking for a pub out in the middle of nowhere.

Finally, on December 2, we got orders to move across the channel. We left as a convoy for the port of Plymouth where we boarded LSTs in the afternoon. The channel was pretty rough, so we had to wait until the next day. We spent the night sleeping where we could. There was a Mexican-American fellow in another battery who was from San Jose, California, and formerly from Santa Paula. He was very good at imitating Frank Sinatra; and that night, I could hear him singing somewhere in the boat, which helped me stop thinking about whatever lay ahead of us. The next day, December 6, our convoy of loaded ships took off and many of us got really seasick. The LSTs were landing crafts with flat bottoms, which made for a rough trip when riding the waves up and down. We finally arrived at Le Havre, France, and set anchor overnight. The next day, the convoy followed the Seine River, which was smooth and lined with beautiful towns on both sides of the river. Our destination was the river port of Rouen, which had been the target of many bombings by U.S. and British planes. There was devastation everywhere with only a few buildings still standing.

After disembarking, we were assigned to a small village called Totes, a few miles north of Rouen. Our battery was directed to a muddy apple orchard. Nearby, were old launching pads, which the Germans had used for some of their rockets. We pitched our two-man tents in the midst of the muddy orchard. I recall going to the nearby village and buying a big loaf of French bread, which I used for a pillow.

One afternoon, a really pretty French girl came by and started to talk to me. She invited me to go visit her at a nearby village, and I agreed to a date. Her name was Bernadette. That evening, I invited one of my friends to go with me and when we reached the village, I went to a house, which I thought was Bernadette's house. I knocked on the door, and a lady opened the door to peek out. I asked her if Bernadette was in, and she slammed the door shut. We continued down the street; and then, we heard a big commotion, so we headed in the direction of what appeared to be male voices. The voices turned out to be from a group of soldiers from our battalion who had also been invited on a date by Bernadette. It turned that Bernadette was the whore of the village. After a good laugh, we headed back to our muddy camp. We remained there until December 24. That day, we were told that we had been assigned to the Ninth Army, which was stationed along the Dutch-German border. That evening, our tractors, cannons and crews were loaded on tank retrievers (low-bed trucks), for the long trip into the Ninth Army sector.

We began moving through the northern part of France toward the southern part of Belgium. That first night, we could hear the sounds of the Battle of the Bulge, which was raging at its height. We stopped for a break at a town in Belgium where the people were celebrating Christmas Eve. They invited us to share their food, which included stuffed chicken gizzards. After a few moments of fun, we continued on our trip to the front lines.

We arrived the next morning at our destination, which was near a small town in Germany called Ubach. The next day, we were assigned to a position in occupied Siersdorf, a small town that was completely destroyed by Allied bombings. The snow was about six inches deep and as we were setting up our cannons, a German bomber came by and dropped a couple of bombs near our position. That night, I asked myself, *Will I still be here tomorrow?* It seemed that we were there forever as the U.S. Army prepared for the crossing of the Rohr River. At night, the Germans would fire flares in an attempt to see us and we, in turn, would shoot at their river barges and troop concentrations. Since the range of our guns was twenty-five miles, we as a gun crew never knew who or what our shells were hitting. We just fired as directed by our observation command ahead of us. I slept in a foxhole that some infantry guy had dug out. I could tell that he had received a fruitcake for Christmas because there were cake crumbs all over the foxhole. They tasted pretty good, too. One morning as I was returning to our gun installation, after breakfast, two German fighter planes flew by really low and strafed our gun positions. The bullets struck just in front of me, and I barely managed to jump into a nearby foxhole. In a few seconds, they made a U-turn and made a second pass. Fortunately, no one got hurt. That was my first experience of being shot at.

Every evening, a German reconnaissance plane nicknamed Bed Check Charlie would drop a load of bombs wherever the Germans thought we were. They missed most of the time. Every gun installation had a telephone where orders were received for firing the guns, and one of the men was responsible for managing the phone. One night, a Mexican-American gun crew member who was in charge of our phone found out that another Mexican-American was in charge of the phone in another battery. So he called him, and they began to converse in Spanish with each other until the voice of the commander came on loud and clear saying, "Cut the bullshit!" And everything immediately went silent. The rest of us started to laugh. The laughter broke the tense moments of waiting.

The night finally came on February 23, 1944, when the army was ready to cross the Rohr River, which was one of the two main barriers into the heart of Germany. The other was the Rhine River. We hadn't realized how many large cannons were lined up along the front until the evening the firing order came. It became the biggest concentration of artillery firing ever experienced in a war. We could see flashes of firing guns as far as the eye could see. The earth began to tremble as if an earthquake was taking place, and the sky was full of tracer bullets all heading toward the front. While this barrage was going on, the infantry was building pontoon bridges and crossing the river. We were on our way to the heart of Germany. The next day, we crossed the Rohr River at Baal and pushed on until we came to a farm where there was some resistance from the enemy. We pulled into a field, which turned out to be quite muddy, and our tractors got stuck. At that point, the Germans thought that they had us, so they began to fire their most feared cannons—the

88s—at us. I remember a shell landing near us. As I hit the ground, my sergeant hit the ground too with a whimper because he thought we didn't have a chance of surviving. Somehow, we managed to place our guns and make the enemy retreat.

The next morning our kitchen was established in a farm house nearby. There was a path to the farmhouse, and midway along the path was a dead German who looked like a farmer. There was a tobacco pipe lying next to his body and the pockets of his pants and coat had been pulled out by some infantry guy who had killed him and then searched him for valuables.

When we pulled out of the farmhouse area, we passed the guns that had fired at us. The Germans had intended to blow up their guns as they retreated, but apparently, were forced to move so suddenly that they left their cannons with sticks of un-ignited dynamite wrapped around them. We then got onto an autobahn congested with all kinds of military vehicles. In front of us was a truck loaded with boxes of supplies. The driver of the tractor that was pulling our gun pulled close to the slow moving truck and our sergeant jumped over to the truck. He then handed us a couple of boxes, which turned out to contain canned peaches. We enjoyed canned peaches for a long time.

Our tractor had a machine gun opening on the roof which was near the exhaust pipe. The exhaust pipe was big and got really hot. It provided a perfect surface to cook on so we always carried a frying pan with us. Whenever we came to a farm, the first thing we would look for were eggs. Many of the farms had cured legs of ham which we would take along with a big basket of eggs, which we fried on the exhaust pipe.

In April, we were near the Rhine River. I remember that on a Sunday morning, which could have been Easter Sunday, our sergeant went to a Catholic church service, and I went with him. I wasn't much of a church-goer. I can only remember attending two Catholic services in my life besides my baptism as a baby. The service I attended with my sergeant was the last Catholic church service I ever attended. However, I was very conscious of God; and in fact, one of my desires was that I would never have to kill another human being with my rifle. I am grateful that I never had to do so although I'll never know how many German soldiers or civilians died while I was pulling the lanyard of my cannon.

After crossing the Rhine River at Wesel, the rat race for Berlin started. The tractors that pulled our cannons, which traveled at speeds of thirty-five miles an hour, began to move us very quickly towards our destination. Sometimes, we found ourselves in front of the infantry. At one time, we moved eighty-one miles in one day on our way to Berlin, which brought our battalion to a position where we served as support for a joint airborne-and-armored assault on the city of Münster.

A few days later while getting into position at Friedrichhole, which was on the west bank of the Weser River, things got hot. The hottest center of action was a town called Arnum. After our unit had by-passed pockets of German resistance, we came to a farm with many haystacks. As we started to position our guns, the Germans who had been watching us cut loose with their 88 cannons. Shells began exploding overhead. Some of us panicked. I remember running to bury myself under a haystack nearby, but at the same time, I heard the sergeant's voice hollering to come back and set the gun into position. It took about ten minutes to get the gun ready to fire, and all this time, shrapnel was flying all over the place. In fact, a shell landed about five feet from our battery officer who was giving us directions; and fortunately for him and us, the shell did not explode. Later on, another shell fell on the camouflage of one of our guns and also failed to explode. Out of two direct hits—two duds! Somebody must have been wearing a rabbit's foot. We finished setting our guns and began firing at a very short distance because the Germans were just across the field from us. We managed to silence their guns, and then, we began acting as infantry as we flushed out some of the Germans soldiers who were hiding in a farmhouse across a plowed field. We spread out, and one German soldier in a foxhole kept shooting at us, but one of our men tossed a hand grenade and blew him up.

To the right, where I was advancing, a German soldier came out of another foxhole and immediately threw his helmet to the ground, raising a white flag as he ran towards us. Another soldier and I reached the farmhouse. As we went around the back of the building, to our surprise, there were about fifteen German soldiers hiding inside. The moment they saw us, they surrendered. We asked them to drop their rifles and place their hand grenades on a table, and then took them as prisoners. By that time, a sergeant and other soldiers came by and helped us gather the prisoners. As we lined them up and started to march them to a nearby village where our guns were in place, some of our soldiers began to strip the prisoners of their watches, rings, and any other valuables they carried. I personally found that action very distasteful, but there was nothing I could do. After that bit of action, we continued our move towards Berlin.

One night as we reached a small village, we were asked to position our cannons for a possible enemy attack. We were told that we would be firing around every ten minutes that night. The word came, "Prepare for firing!" A few minutes later, the order would be, "Cease firing." And that's the way it was most of the night. I had an army cot, which I placed near the gun so I could try to sleep a little between firing calls. At one point while I was lying down on my cot, one of our crew members, a guy from Santa Paula, came over with his carbine hanging from his shoulder. As he passed by me, he accidentally pulled the trigger of his rifle, and the bullet missed my head by inches.

A similar accident happened to me during an overnight stop at a farm. One of our men had stopped a German truck loaded with crates of bottled gin, and had commanded the driver to drive the truck to where we were located. With the help of others, we unloaded the truck, and everybody took a case of gin. That night, everybody got drunk including me. After drinking the gin, I went rummaging through a farmhouse looking for canned meats and fruits. While in the farmhouse, I accidentally pulled the trigger of my carbine, which was hanging from my shoulder. It narrowly missed my right foot. I was never good at handling hard liquor.

After advancing toward the Elbe River, which was our last obstacle on our way to Berlin, our battalion was temporarily attached to the 5th Armored Division. The reason for this was that the Germans, who were running away from the Russian army, crossed the river to our side and surrendered to us. At one point, units of the Ninth Army met units of the Russian army at the Elbe River. The end of the war was in sight.

On May 6, 1945, the 261st Artillery Battalion was moved back 108 miles to the rear to assume military government duties in the vicinity of Wathlingen. On May 8, word came that hostilities had ended. The following day was officially declared V-E Day. The war in Europe was over.

Another move on May 11 took our unit to the vicinity of Braunschwieg for occupation duties. The batteries were scattered throughout the surrounding villages where schools, apartments, and private homes were taken over for use as military quarters. From then on, training schedules became the order of the day.

On June 24, the 261st Artillery Battalion moved into the Seventh Army sector in the American Occupation Zone, some two hundred miles to the south. Here again, our unit assumed military-government duties with headquarters in Wachtersbach. Battery B, to which I belonged, was placed at Schlierbach, a small village located in a beautiful valley surrounded by lush forests. Four of us took over a private home for our quarters. The lady who lived there had to go elsewhere. She used to come every day to tend her garden, but she could not go into the house. We were under strict orders not to socialize with the German people, which was easier said than done. Near the house where I was staying, there was a two-story house with a large window. One time, I saw a pretty girl standing by the window and I went out to wave at her, but she immediately looked the other way. After that, I began to use my binoculars, and she knew I was watching her window so she would peek out and then hide. I never could make a connection with her. The village was untouched by the war. I remember going on a day pass to Frankfurt, which was about an hour's drive. Most of the city was devastated by all the bombings.

Our officers were staying at a big mansion, which had a cellar with different kinds of wines and champagne. On one occasion, our battery had a victory party, and cases of wine from the mansion were brought out, and we had a ball. On June 22, 1945, the battalion held a review, and some awards were made. This was the last formation for us as a unit. Transfers then began. Those eligible for discharge under the point system were placed in units that became homebound.

On Friday, July 13, word came that the remaining members of our unit would be going back to the United States. We were taken by a truck convoy to Camp Lucky Strike near Paris, France. For the first time, I had the opportunity to visit Paris, which was a six and a half hour drive away. I remember going to see the Eiffel Tower and getting lost in the metro. I had a few drinks of cognac as well. After ten days, we were loaded again on trucks and taken to the port of Le Havre where a liberty ship, the USS *Leonard*, was waiting to take us out to sea and then home. Those of us who did not have enough points for discharge were to train in the United States before going to fight the Japanese. After a few days at sea, we heard that Japan had surrendered, and a big "Hurrah!" was heard.

We spent thirteen days aboard ship, and I was seasick all the way. Just the smell coming from inside the ship made me throw up. I spent the whole voyage on the deck of the ship, sleeping under a heavy canvas. I remember lying on my back on the deck, and looking up, I could see the ship's mast going up and down, up and down and that made my stomach turn inside out. At the end of the voyage, my six-foot-one frame still weighed only 133 lbs.

Upon our arrival at Newport News, Virginia, we were met by an army band with a big sign welcoming our battalion home. We were then convoyed to Camp Patrick Henry where we were processed, and those of us from the Pacific Coast boarded a Pullman train bound for San Pedro, California. After a forty-five-day furlough, seventy percent of our battalion reported back to Camp Bowie, Texas, where the 261st Field Artillery Battalion became a regular army unit. Those of us in the remaining thirty percent were to be discharged. A few weeks later, we were shipped to Fort Sam Houston for processing and discharge. The night prior to our discharge, we were given a pass, and we all went to town. I must have drunk a lot of beer because I passed out on the bus that took us back to the camp. The following day, we were honorably discharged from the U.S. Army and were given three hundred dollars in cash and a train ticket home. Our discharge was effective November 17, 1945. Adios, U.S. Army life!

Members of 261ˢᵗ Field Artillery Battalion - Battery B.
Albino - Second Row, Second from left, kneeling

Albino R. Pineda

Barton on the Sea - New Hamilton, England
Old Hotel used as temporary quarters for Battery B

*Germany - Albino with
jeep driver*

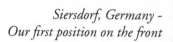

*Siersdorf, Germany -
Our first position on the front*

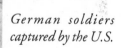

*German soldiers
captured by the U.S.*

*Half of gun crew -
at war's end*

Return to USA

Privates first class -
John Rivera and Albino

Arrival at Newport News, Virginia

Occupied Germany - Albino

Chapter XIV

BACK TO CIVILIAN LIFE

After arriving at my sister Dolores's home and visiting my girlfriend, I returned to Nogales, Mexico, for a few days. Meanwhile, my mother had applied for a permanent U.S. resident visa at the American consulate in Nogales, Mexico. While I was there, she received her visa. I went back to Santa Paula and my mother and brothers Tony and Isidro, my niece Dora, and my nephew Amador followed later on. My future mother-in-law, who had a strong liking for me, offered to rent my mother an apartment that was very close to her house. I continued living with my sister Lola and her family.

A few days after my return to Santa Paula, I went to work as a temporary longshoreman at nearby Port Hueneme, California, unloading cement bags from ships that were returning with material that had been intended for the war front. As time passed, the ships began to arrive less frequently, and all temporary longshoremen were laid off. It had been a good paying job. As the days went by, I began to notice that I was developing a serious case of sinus problems. My nose was always plugged, so the doctor gave me some nose drops that shrank my nose membranes but, at the same time, made me very nervous.

Sometime later, I went to work for a lemon packing house in Santa Paula. My job was picking up boxes of lemons and emptying them onto a moving conveyor. It was a back-breaking job because I had to stay apace in feeding the fast-moving conveyor that moved the fruit to the women sorters. The pay was fifty-five cents an hour. After working there a few months, some of the workers got a raise of five cents, but I, along with others, did not receive a raise because I had not worked there long enough. Since the work was very difficult and since I didn't receive a raise, I quit my job.

Shortly after, I joined the Common Laborer's Union. When there was a job, the pay was a dollar and fifteen cents an hour, but the work was never steady. Sometimes, I had to go and pick tomatoes in between jobs. At one point, the union sent me to work for a pipeline company that was laying a gas line between Santa Paula and Castaic. My job was to dig trenches with a pick and a shovel. The good thing about the union was that we got paid time and a half for overtime and Saturdays. One could always tell which workers were war veterans because we all wore khaki pants and shirts, green trench jackets, and army combat boots.

During this time, I continued to go out with my girlfriend, Naomi. In fact, we were making plans to marry. When we set the date for our wedding, she asked me to go to her parents and ask for her hand. I recall the night I went to talk to her parents. When I walked in, her parents were sitting at their dining table, and her father was counting the day's receipts from their grocery store. As I started to talk, I directed my words at him because I thought it would be difficult for him to say yes. I remember saying, "As you know, Naomi and I have been dating for a long time. So we have decided to get married and I have come tonight to ask you for her hand."

He kept on counting money like he had not heard what I had said. At that point, my future mother-in-law, who liked me, interjected, saying, "Oh, I think they will do all right. It's going to be hard at the beginning, but I think the Lord is going to bless them eventually." As I walked out, I don't recall if my future father-in-law said anything. All I remember is that I came out feeling that it was okay for us to get married. This happened around June 1946, almost six months after I was discharged from the army.

We set August 11 as the date for our wedding. Naomi always told the story that I had said, "We better get married on that date or else I will go and blow every penny I have saved up to now." That was a standing joke because all I had saved was three hundred dollars.

As it got closer to our wedding date, I was digging trenches for a gas pipeline company along the highway between Santa Paula and Fillmore. The day that Naomi took the Greyhound bus to Los Angeles to buy her wedding dress, other laborers and I were digging a manhole right next to the roadway near the railroad crossing by Sespe Ranch, which is about six miles east of Santa Paula. On the return trip to Santa Paula, the greyhound bus would make a stop before crossing the tracks, right next to where we were digging. In the late afternoon as I was shoveling dirt out of the manhole, I saw the Greyhound bus coming west, so I knew Naomi would be on board. When the bus neared the side of the trench, I ducked down so no one could see me. I didn't want Naomi to say, "That's my future husband shoveling dirt out of that trench." We used to laugh about that years later.

Chapter XV

MY MARRIAGE

On August 11, 1946, I wore a rented tuxedo, and the rest of the wedding participants were also elegantly dressed for the ceremony. My best man, the maid of honor, and the others were all close friends of Naomi. Since I had just become a Protestant, we chose to hold our ceremony at the First Presbyterian Church of Santa Paula. Prior to the wedding, Naomi's father had invited some people to a luncheon at Lin's Chinese Restaurant, which was right next door to his store. When it came time for him to walk the bride to the altar, he did it jovially. Naomi would be the first of his five daughters to get married.

Just before the wedding, a problem developed. It was a hot day, and there was no ice for the punch that would be served at the reception. We looked everywhere and couldn't find any ice. Because it was Sunday, the ice factory by the railroad tracks on Mill Street was closed. As we searched for ice, we saw Don Amado, an old man who made a living selling snow cones from a wagon. He had a big piece of ice so we began to try to convince him to sell us his chunk of ice. He said no because he could make more money selling snow cones, and he needed the money. Finally, we told him we would pay him whatever he thought the ice was worth. Reluctantly, he thought about it and agreed to sell us the piece of ice. That saved the day.

We were married by Reverand Luis P. Tirre who had been the minister of the Union Spanish Mission for many years and who was well known throughout the community.

After the wedding and reception, Naomi and I had to leave because my uncle Joe Rivera, who lived in Los Angeles, was going to give us a ride to downtown Los Angeles (of all places) where we were going to spend our honeymoon. We borrowed my father-in-law's car to go to his house to change and wait for our ride. As we drove to the house, Naomi sat in the front seat with me. One of the old ladies from the church had asked us to give her a ride to her house, which was a few doors from my in-laws so she rode in the back seat. We started to honk the horn in celebration of our marriage but people looked at us in confusion because there was an old lady sitting in the back seat. Soon, we were on our way to Los Angeles in my uncle's car. He took us to the Stilwell Hotel, which was on Broadway in the downtown area. We spent our honeymoon going to shows, and on one of the nights, we went to the Hollywood Palladium where Les Brown and his orchestra were playing. We went in and not being a good dancer, I chickened out and told my bride, "It's too crowded."

After that, she couldn't stop laughing. "Do you want the whole floor for ourselves?" she asked. To my relief, we didn't dance. I recall that by some coincidence I met an army buddy who was vacationing in Los Angeles and was staying at the same hotel. We agreed to meet the following night to go out for dinner together, but the next day, we got so excited about some shows we were going to see that we failed to keep our date with my friend. I never saw him again.

While in Los Angeles, I bought some pajamas, slippers, a robe, and other things. On our way back after our honeymoon, I placed them in the overhead compartment of the bus we were riding in and when we arrived in Santa Paula, we got off and forgot the box with all my new clothes. This was a big loss for us because we didn't have very much money.

Back in Santa Paula, we lived a few weeks at my in-laws' house. Naomi had four sisters, five brothers and a cousin. With the exception of two, they all lived at home. After several weeks, Naomi's oldest half brother, Tino, who owned a small rental house on North Oak street, told us that the house was available for us to rent. We rented it for fourteen dollars a month. It was a one-bedroom house with really tiny rooms. The front room was so tiny that all we could place there was a love seat and a chair. At the back of the small kitchen was a porch where we were able to put a small icebox and a hand-wringing style washing machine. My work at that time was anything but steady. Naomi, who had gone to a beauty school in Los Angeles, had a part-time job so together we made enough to pay the rent and buy food. We continued to work and save whatever we could.

When we got married, we had no idea how many children we wanted. We just knew that they would eventually come. A few weeks after our honeymoon, we discovered that Naomi was pregnant.

I kept working on and off. And while most of my jobs were of short duration, we were somehow able to live a happy and comfortable life. A few months into our marriage, I received a card from the army accounting office saying that the government had overpaid my family allowance by 150 dollars, and I had so many days to reimburse them. That was a blow to our meager finances, but we repaid it.

As my work was sporadic, I became accustomed to applying for unemployment benefits. I remember once being unemployed for nine weeks straight. For some reason or another, I didn't receive any unemployment checks until finally, on the ninth week, I received nine unemployment checks. Good thing we could buy groceries on credit at my in-laws' grocery store.

My sinus problem, meanwhile, had turned into a serious asthma condition. I remember waking up at midnight gasping for air because my chest would just tighten up, preventing me from breathing normally. At one time, in desperation, I went to a clinic in Los Angeles where they washed my colon out and put me on a cleansing diet. I tried that a few times, but my asthma continued without improvement. I was very skinny, and I remember sending for the Charles Atlas correspondence course on bodybuilding. In spite of my health condition, I was anxious to gain weight and develop my body. I was a milk drinker, and ate good meals but still could not gain weight. Working in construction and under extremely dusty conditions made my asthma worse.

I had never been a member of a church until I met Naomi. Although I came from a Catholic background, I thought churches were simply places one attended on Sunday mornings with no strings attached. As I began to attend Naomi's church and to get involved in the activities of the congregation, I discovered that the congregation is an extended family where "family love" is shared. Naomi had been active in the young people's league so I became involved as well. However, my involvement soon transitioned into a more serious leadership role in the church. We both became very active, which turned out to be a blessing for our marriage. In spite of my health problems, I was active and enjoying several leadership roles in the church. I was discovering talents that I didn't know I had—talents that were being developed, which later on would help me in my secular and community work and, many years later, in my role as a professional in the larger church organization.

One day, I got a call from the union hall that a job was available so I took it. I was sent to work for contractors who were beginning to build the Matilija Dam above Ojai. My first two days of work consisted of unloading loose bulk cement from a railroad boxcar with a big shovel-like device. The device was pulled with a cable toward a dump truck, which in turn carried the cement to the dam site. I don't know how I, as an asthmatic young man, was able to survive doing that kind of work. After that, I was sent to the dam to push a wheelbarrow full of concrete up a ramp eight hours a day. Tough work, but I did it. After all, I had a wife and a future child to support. Next, I became a driller, which paid a little more. I was making a dollar and sixty-five cents an hour. We were actually functioning as miners because we were drilling and dynamiting deep shafts into the mountainside that would be filled with concrete to prevent water seepage through the fractured rock formations. I was put on the night shift.

Naomi Salas Pineda

*In-laws - Juan G and
Concepcion M. Salas*

*My Wedding: Daniel Lujan, Oton Lujan, Best Man - Happy Sonora, Albino,
Naomi, Maid of Honor - Estella Garcia, Fortuna Limon, and Loretta Romero*

Concepcion M. Salas, Albino, Naomi, My Mother

Albino, far left, working with crew at Matilija Dam

Chapter XVI

BIRTH OF OUR FIRST CHILD

Meanwhile, Naomi was getting closer to her due date and had temporarily quit her part-time job at the beauty shop. During one of those nights that I was coming home at midnight, I was told that Naomi had given birth to a baby boy weighing five pounds and five ounces—a tiny baby. We were both very happy that we finally had a son but we needed a name for him. Naomi's suggestion was that we name him Johnnie after her oldest brother who was killed in an auto accident on his way home in 1945 while on army furlough. My suggestion was that as a family tradition the name Albino or Albina should be used in each generation of my family. Somehow, we ended up with a compromise. We named him Johnnie Al.

Our joy was not for long. About a week after his birth, we discovered that our baby could not hold down his food. One day, he got so sick that we quickly put him in a buggy and ran down the street to my mother-in-law's. She told us to rush him to the doctor who, after several tests, determined that we should take him to the hospital right away. He suspected that there was a defect in our baby's stomach valve that required surgery. The doctor suggested that we take him to Santa Barbara Cottage Hospital, which we did. The hospital doctors confirmed that Johnnie Al needed immediate surgery to correct his stomach valve. I was asked to give blood for the operation. As inexperienced parents, Naomi and I were frantic. After the surgery, the doctors assured us that he would be all right. A week later, we brought our baby home. From then on, he was fine and no longer rejected his food. I continued working nights at Matilija Dam. Naomi stayed home taking care of our son.

One day, I learned that my half-sister Josefa, who had recently arrived from Arizona, had been shot by her drunken husband while in a rage. He shot her with a small rifle, and the bullet got lodged in her spine, which paralyzed her from the waist down. Josefa remained paralyzed for the rest of her life. Her husband was sent to prison for a year. They had eight children—Arthur, Elvira, Theodore, Freddie, Nicacia, Frances, Manuel, and Rosie. Theodore got killed by an exploding shell while serving in the Korean War.

As I continued to work, we were able to buy a used car, which we needed badly. A few weeks after I bought the car, I was driving home from Ventura on Highway 126. I was traveling at around forty-five miles an hour, and it was drizzling. My rear tires were bald. Suddenly, my car started to fishtail. Being inexperienced at the wheel, I panicked. Instead of taking my foot off the throttle, I stepped on it and the car spun around, and rolled over onto a freshly plowed field. The car landed on the passenger side. I crawled out, and other motorists stopped to help me get my car upright. Even as scared as I was, I drove the rest of the way home with a big dent on the passenger side of the muddy car.

When I got home, I took a hose and washed the car down and then told Naomi what had happened. She looked at the car and started to cry because she said I could have been seriously hurt. Later on, I took the car to a body repair shop where they smoothed out the dent. After that experience, I regularly checked my tires for wear.

On May 14, 1948, my work at the dam ended and I went back to the union hall to make myself available for another job. In August of that same year, Naomi started to work again while my mother took care of our son. I landed a job working with a bunch of men from Santa Paula, including my youngest brother, Isidro, who also belonged to the union. We worked for a contractor who was building a road up the mountain across the highway from Point Mugu. The road was being built to create access to a radar station that would eventually be built on top of the mountain. We were clearing the brush (which was infested with rattlesnakes) so that the bulldozers could cut the roadway. That work lasted for a while. The contractor owned a twin-engined

Cessna airplane and when he came to the job, he would always fly around a couple of times before landing at Point Mugu. We always knew it was him. His brother, a very bright man, was in charge of the jobs. I fell into their good graces as I will explain later. It was during this time that my oldest half sister, Lucy, moved to Santa Paula from Tijuana after having received her permanent residence visa. Around this same time, we formally presented our baby son to the church so his name would be in the church records.

Earlier in the year, I had started attending night school at Ventura Junior College. My niece Dora, Naomi's cousin Tita Favila, and I took English classes. I was also studying for my GED. After school ended, I took the GED test and passed it. The college gave me my high school diploma which represented a very gratifying moment for me. I continued to take other classes including a real estate principles class.

In August of 1949, I began teaching Sunday school and also became a foreman at my job for the first time. That same month, the remains of my nephew Jesus "Johnny" Chavez finally arrived from the Philippines where he had been killed during World War II on one of the islands. He was buried in Santa Paula.

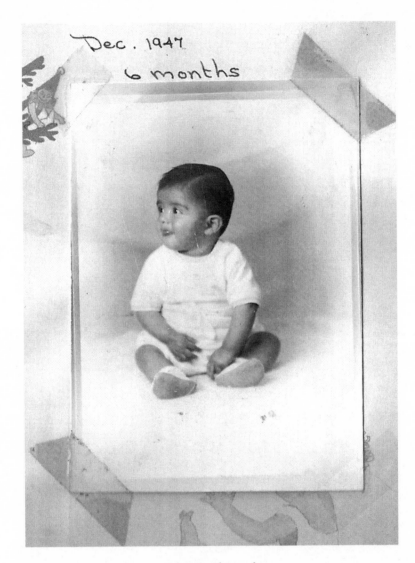

Johnnie Al Pineda

Johnnie Al Pineda

Chapter XVII

ABOUT NAOMI'S BIRTH
AND CITIZENSHIP

Back in 1923, when my parents-in-law were expecting the birth of their second child, my mother-in-law decided she wanted the child to be born in Mexico (contrary to today's practices by Mexican people) so her mother could help her with the birth. Consequently, that child, who was Naomi, was born in Torreón, Coahuila, Mexico, on December 11, 1923. When she was only a few weeks old, she was brought home to Santa Paula. Having been born in Mexico, baby Naomi was now a Mexican citizen. After we got married, she began to work on her citizenship papers, and on December 9, 1949, she officially became an American citizen. It was around that time that Dr. Artemas Strong became our family doctor.

Chapter XVIII

TIMES OF FEAR AND INSECURITY

The year 1950 came around, and it was during those years that people were concerned about the cold war. The threat of the Soviet Union was always on our minds. People were building bomb shelters, and there was the constant fear of a nuclear attack on the United States. One evening, we were in our little cottage when a strong earthquake began to shake our house, and a light transformer near our house blew up with a bang. A strong, blinding light lit up the night. We thought that it was an atom bomb that had exploded and in a flash, we were inside a closet waiting for the house to blow up. After a few minutes, we came out, and everything was dark and quiet. I went outside, and the neighbors told me that the big bang was the transformer that had blown out in front of our house.

That scare left me really spooked. Wherever I went, I was afraid that there was going to be a big explosion. That feeling of fear and insecurity lasted for a long time.

One morning, I was driving to my job in Thousand Oaks. When I got to Camarillo, I saw a truck and a trailer that had for some reason gone off the road. Apparently, the driver had tried to jump out of the cab but, unfortunately, as he tried to jump out, the truck struck a palm tree on the driver's side and crushed the driver. The upper part of his body was hanging down from the cab door. His face looked gray and lifeless. Seeing the dead man made my feelings of insecurity even worse. That feeling of insecurity lasted for about two years.

I also remember getting my first traffic ticket. Our son was two and a half years old, and one day, I took him to Ventura. As I approached California Street on Thompson Boulevard, I was in the slow lane. When Johnnie Al saw the beach, he asked if we could go to the beach. I told my son we could go and I made a reckless left turn without seeing a police car that was two cars behind me. When I made the left turn, the police officer came behind me and stopped me. He gave me my first traffic ticket for making an unsafe turn. The fine was five dollars. To this writing, I have only received four wrong turn citations, and the last one was twenty-eight years ago.

The year 1950 was not a very good year at my in-laws' grocery store. My father-in-law was having problems paying the store bills. Consequently, he asked Naomi and me if we wanted to buy a 1949 Chevrolet sedan that his son Sam had left behind when he was shipped by the army to Korea. We needed a good car, so we bought it from him. It was a very nice-looking car with low mileage. I sold my other used car to my brother Tony.

Chapter XIX

WORKING AWAY FROM HOME

Attending church regularly was a great blessing for our lives. When I first joined the church, I was named Sunday school superintendent, which was the beginning of my development as a church leader. I also began to lead worship services for the first time. As time went on, Naomi and I became quite involved in the church. It was good for us.

On April 2, 1950, I received a call from the contractor I had worked for building the road up the mountain just east of Point Mugu who I will hereinafter refer to as "David". He wanted me to work for him while his company built a right-of-way for a pipeline that would run from West Palm Springs to La Puente. I gladly accepted the offer in spite of the fact that it was out of the county. Since the pipeline would cut across many properties, backyards, corrals, farms, and fields, my job was to build gates or fences so the machines could come through. I drove a truck loaded with fence posts, rolls of barbwire, and lumber to build gates of different kinds and sizes.

I rented a motel in Banning and later, Naomi and our son joined me. Behind the motel, about an eighth of a mile, were the railroad tracks where long freight trains went by in both directions all day. Our son used to stand by a fence and watch the long trains chugging up the grade, throwing a long stream of black smoke. Banning, at the time, was just a small town surrounded by desert. I really enjoyed my work. Cutting fences across private backyards and farms was interesting work. Besides, I was my own boss. As the work moved west, we kept moving to towns like Ontario then Pomona. One evening, we went to have dinner at a Mexican restaurant; and lo and behold, it was owned and operated by Santa Paulan, Don Juan Munoz. We became regulars at his eatery as Naomi knew the family really well.

One of our bulldozer operators had a Piper Cub airplane, and he took me for my first airplane ride. Later on, on another occasion, my boss who owned the twin-engined Cessna took Naomi, our son, another person, and me for a ride. It was nighttime, and he let Naomi sit at the co-pilot's seat. At one point, he asked my wife to take the controls. She grabbed the controls but didn't know what to do, so she just froze and kept going in a circle. That was an experience she never forgot. I only worked for a few months on that job.

Before my Pomona job ended, Naomi and our son returned to Santa Paula. The fellow who owned the Piper Cub lived in Thousand Oaks and I remember he offered to fly me to Fillmore one Friday night. There was a weedy landing strip across the river in Fillmore so he said he would drop me there, and Naomi could come and pick me up. I accepted the lift, and we took off from Banning after work. It was late, but there was still some daylight left. As we flew, he followed the highway for direction. However, as we passed San Bernardino, we noticed that a fog bank was rolling in. Soon, we hit the fog, and he lost sight of the highway. He kept on flying until, all of a sudden we saw the side of a mountain. He quickly banked the plane to the left and managed to make a U-turn, barely in time to avoid hitting the mountain. We continued in the other direction, and luckily, we saw both daylight and the highway once again. He started to follow the highway at a lower altitude to miss the fog. We were finally able to land in Fillmore where I got off. I remember being so thrilled about flying in a plane that I didn't even get upset over the near crash. I didn't tell Naomi about the incident because I knew she would get very upset about it.

We always remembered Banning because, on weekends, we would drive to Palm Springs, Borrego Springs, and other desert areas to see different kinds of cactus plants and flowers. On one occasion, we went to see the play *Ramona* at the Hemet Bowl.

After the Banning/Pomona job ended, I came back to Santa Paula and worked on and off in different construction jobs. The year 1951 came, and we had saved $2,247 with no outstanding debts. Soon after, David got a contract to build a roadway in Santa Margarita, just north of San Luis Obispo. David had been a pilot for the publisher of one of Los Angeles' largest newspapers. He was a good pilot although he liked to drink a lot. I went to Santa Margarita to work for David and took my brother Tony with me. I was the laborer's foreman, and my job was to install corrugated metal drain pipes of different sizes wherever creeks crossed the roadway. I was good at drilling and using dynamite to cut rocky banks whenever the road needed widening.

David's brother, whose name I have forgotten, was job superintendent and was one of the finest persons I had ever met—always amiable and ready to tell a good joke. The only bad thing was that he had lost his wife which affected him a great deal. In fact, he developed suicidal tendencies. One morning, someone went to his motel room and discovered that he had turned the gas valve of an unlit heater on. They were able to get him out just in time to save his life. After working there a few weeks, I was asked to do drilling and dynamiting in an open pit iron mine, some twenty miles east of Lucerne Valley. The open pit mine was on top of a hill that was in the middle of nowhere. One could look as far as the eye could see and not see a tree. It was just a plain desert. The heat rose over a hundred degrees every day. My job was to drill fifty-foot holes into the iron ore, load them with dynamite, and set them off. We would then dig out the broken iron rock and load it onto trucks with a large mechanical shovel. The ore was then trucked to the nearest railroad site for shipment.

Eventually, Naomi, our son, and one of Naomi's younger brothers, joined me when I rented a small house in Lucerne Valley, which consisted of a few houses and a couple of grocery stores. There was also a small clothing and general store owned by a Frenchman named Rene Belbenoit who was selling a book entitled *I Escaped from Devil's Island*. The book told the true story of how he had escaped from Devil's Island. He sold me a copy of his book and autographed it for me.

It was during that job that we received the news that David's brother had succeeded in committing suicide. My brother Tony, who had stayed in Santa Margarita, was on the job when he heard a loud explosion, which came from the area where boxes of dynamite and fuses were stored. He ran and when he got there, to his horror, he saw what had happened. David's brother had taken a stick of dynamite and an electrical fuse, and put them together. He had then put the stick of dynamite inside his hat, and put it on. He lifted the hood of his Cadillac and connected the fuse wire to the battery terminal. It blew off his head and part of his upper torso. According to my brother Tony, there were pieces of brain and flesh hanging from the branches of nearby oak trees.

Meanwhile, after we stripped the iron mine, we went to Tonopah, Nevada, in preparation for building a road up a mountain about sixty miles northeast of Tonopah. We stayed about three days in a downtown hotel in the old mining town while the equipment arrived. I remember clearly the first day when we drove up and stopped to have lunch at a restaurant. We had sleeping bags and supplies in the back seat of my boss's car. It was very hot, and we had all the windows down. When we stopped to have lunch, I asked my boss if I should close the windows since we had all our stuff in the car. He replied, "Al, you have to learn to trust people. No one is going to steal our things." I said, "Okay," and we went into the restaurant to eat. When we came out, half of our stuff was gone. He didn't say a word and neither did I. When we finally got to the job site, we were ready to cut a road along the side of a high mountain where there was a large deposit of tungsten ore, which was in very high demand in those days. We worked for about a week and carved a crude road, but before we reached the top, the man who was funding the project failed to pay David any money for the work we had already completed. Difficulties had arisen, and we were told that there was no money available after all for the project. At the time, we were sleeping in sleeping bags out in the open. The valley at the foot of the mountains was very green and literally swarming with jackrabbits. The coyotes that came around were fat because there was so much prey around. David had flown his plane to a makeshift landing strip behind a restaurant that was in the middle of nowhere. At night, the restaurant had a band that played for passers-by and David, who was good at playing the drums, did so, especially after a few drinks.

The day I was to return home, David—who had been drinking—said he would fly me to Oxnard. There was a young fellow from the area who had injured one of his ankles. He wanted to go to Los Angeles so he also came with us on the plane. We took off from the lot behind the restaurant. I was sitting at the co-pilot's seat. After being in the air for a while, David decided to take a nap to sober up. He asked me to take the controls and just keep the plane steady. I accepted the challenge and became an instant pilot. As I looked ahead, there was a mountain range, so I kept going higher and higher because I wanted to make sure I would clear the mountain top. After about a half hour, David woke up and came over to his pilot seat and exclaimed, "Jesus Christ! Why are you flying so high?" I told him that I didn't like the looks of the mountain top. He took over and brought the plane down to a lower altitude.

When we finally reached South Mountain near Santa Paula on our way to Oxnard, the fuel tank light turned red, and David said, "We can make it to Oxnard." But what he discovered moments later was that there were low clouds, so he headed toward Ventura where he saw a break in the clouds. We barely made it to the Oxnard airport where Naomi was waiting for me. I eventually returned to the job in Santa Margarita. Meanwhile, Naomi was pregnant again with our second child.

Chapter XX

BIRTH OF OUR SECOND CHILD

The morning of December 18, 1951, I got a call that Naomi had given birth to a baby girl at 8:30 a.m. When I heard the news, my boss offered to fly me to Santa Paula, and I excitedly accepted his kind offer. After all, this was our second child and again, I had not been there to support my wife. My boss not only flew me to Santa Paula but also went with me to meet our newborn daughter, Patricia. Patricia was named after the actress Patricia Medina. After seeing that both mother and child were doing fine, I flew back with my boss to San Luis Obispo so I could drive back to Santa Paula and be with my family for the weekend.

I recall that we had just installed our first telephone. Also, we were the first on both sides of the family to buy a used twelve-inch black-and-white television set, which came in a big cabinet. All of our relatives would come to our house to watch TV. I remember staying up most of the night one evening watching swimmer Barbara Chadwick swim across the channel from Catalina Island to the mainland. In those days, the *Spade Cooley* show was very popular on TV.

I continued working in Santa Margarita, and on weekends, I would come home to be with my family. When we finished the road job in April of 1952, I returned home.

David treated me like a son. After I returned home from Santa Margarita, he helped me join the Operating Engineers' Union. He called the union and specifically requested that I be dispatched to a foreman position with his company even though there was no work. In June of 1952, I was initiated into the International Union of Operating Engineers and was dispatched as a heavy-equipment foreman. I was part of a first wave of Hispanics to join this union. Later that month, David called me to say that a friend needed a foreman in the San Fernando Valley. He recommended me, and I was hired. I supervised a few short jobs in the valley, and then, David's friend got a road-paving job on Highway 33 between Ojai and Oak View. During that job, I got a salary increase and stayed with David's contractor friend until the job was complete. But now David wanted me back. He had rented some of his bulldozers to a company that was installing fifteen miles of large pipe to bring water from the Colorado River to San Diego. He wanted me to oversee his equipment, and at the same time, he got me a job as a supervisor for the other company. The job was to last for two years.

I rented an adobe house close to where I would be working and took my wife and two children with me. By then, Naomi's older sister Toni had gotten married to Harold Kennedy, and we let them use our house on Oak Street while we were gone. By that time, our son Johnnie Al was attending school; and our little princess was beginning to learn to walk. The house we rented was right on the pass between Rainbow Valley and the town of Temecula. It was situated at the foot of a mountain that had rocks as big as our house all around and up the mountain. Our house came with a well that provided our drinking water. I was making good money and was home every night enjoying my wife and children. My wife had a car, which she used when she went to buy groceries in Temecula. At that time, Temecula was just a small town with a motel, a restaurant, and a gas station. I drove a jeep that the company furnished me.

We had a Cocker Spaniel named Beany Boy who would run around the house barking his head off when we would return from a trip, perhaps trying to show us that he was taking care of the house. Unfortunately, Naomi got pretty nervous when we lived there because she wasn't used to seeing snakes, lizards, and all the other wild creatures that were in the mountainside and around the house. One evening, we had just gone to bed and turned the light out when she felt something wet drop on her face. She jumped and turned the light on, and we saw a bat flying around in the room. It immediately squeezed itself through a tiny crack in the ceiling. After that, Naomi wouldn't dare sleep with her face uncovered at night.

There were other instances that compounded her nervousness. Our baby daughter used to sleep in a crib by a window facing the road. Across the road was the right-of-way where the pipeline for the water project would run parallel to the road. The house was about four hundred feet from the right-of-way. One day, the contractor's workers were blasting the rocky terrain and when they got to a place in front of our house, they detonated a big blast that shook the house and broke the window near the crib, showering glass all over our baby girl. My wife was infuriated and went over to complain to the superintendent who apologized and sent a carpenter to fix the window.

A few nights later, our baby daughter developed a high fever and began to experience convulsions. Her eyes looked listless, so my wife took her in her arms, and we jumped into the car thinking that she was dying on us. I began to drive toward the town of Fallbrook, which was some fifteen miles away. I was taking the curves on the road at a very high speed. We were both praying and crying while our son Johnnie Al was hanging on for dear life in the back seat, wondering what was happening. We arrived at the hospital, and the personnel there thought we were Native Americans. I told them that we were Mexican-Americans and that we had insurance. I remember seeing them place our baby in a container that had ice in it. They kept her in the hospital until the next day. By then, she was okay. All of these nerve-wrenching experiences caused my wife to suffer a mild nervous breakdown. When the job ended on December 11, 1953, almost two years after it started, we moved back to Santa Paula.

Our baby daughter - Patricia or Patsy as she was called during part of her life - 1953

Chapter XXI

BUYING OUR FIRST HOME

When we returned to Santa Paula from Temecula, we realized that we needed a larger house than the one we had been renting from my brother-in-law. We looked around and found a two-bedroom house on Brett Way in Santa Paula. It had a large fenced backyard, which was perfect. The asking price was eleven thousand dollars with a two thousand dollar down payment, which we were able to make. Prior to buying the house, Naomi had been staying with her parents trying to shake off her nervous breakdown by just relaxing. Our children were growing and we needed more room. After we moved in to our new house, we found the house to be very comfortable. Our children made friends with all the other children in the neighborhood. We enjoyed wonderful times at our Brett way home. We still had our twelve-inch black-and-white TV set, which our children enjoyed, watching television programs such as *Engineer Bill and Sheriff John.*

Shortly after moving into the Brett Way home, I went to work for a friend who had been a mechanic for David's company. He had bought some small Ford tractors and skip loaders which were used to grade around newly built tract homes in the San Fernando Valley. I drove the tractors and graded the yards of some of the first tract homes that were built in the Valley. At that time, San Fernando Valley was being transformed into what it is today. Orange groves were being uprooted to build new tract homes. Freeways were nonexistent in the area. I worked five months all over the Valley, driving home to Santa Paula every day. Driving through Simi Valley, all one could see were tumbleweeds, a church, the Tipsy Fox beer joint, a fire station, and a few ranch houses.

I left the Valley job because my old employer, David, called me to tell me that he had gotten me a foreman's job with the Guy F. Atkinson Company. They were building a section of a levee along the Los Angeles River. He also offered me a room at his house in Paramount so I wouldn't have to pay for a motel. It was a kind gesture that I accepted. He and his wife cared a lot about me. The problem with the job, I later discovered, was that it was very stressful. The scrapers moving the earth from the bottom of the river kept bogging down in the mud and so did the bulldozers that were pushing them. As a consequence, productivity was not what had been expected, and the pressure was on me. Being new to the company, I didn't know any of my co-workers or the supervisors, so I began to feel homesick. As I looked around, the only friendly thing I saw was my car parked nearby. After a month and a half, I quit the job and went back to work for my friend in the Valley although it meant less pay. After a couple of months, the work slowed down, and I went to work for other contractors on short-term jobs.

When I was off work, I enjoyed playing with my children. My son Johnnie Al always wanted me to play ball with him in our backyard while my daughter, a little doll herself, was always drawing dolls on a paper pad. She would talk to her drawings as if they were real. There were times when I could hear her scolding her doll drawings for reasons that only she knew. But most of the time, she would have a group of little neighborhood girls following her as she played the role of teacher.

As the year 1964 rolled on, Naomi and I continued to be active in our church—she as a Sunday school teacher, and I, as a Sunday school superintendent and chair of the Board of Trustees. I then went to work again for my friend in the San Fernando Valley in spite of the long drive. Jobs in the area were very scarce.

A year and a half earlier, a young pastor had been appointed to our church, which consisted of a small wooden chapel. The pastor, Reverand Mardy Olivas, was disappointed when he saw the small church he had been appointed to serve. After getting acquainted with the congregation, he proposed to move forward with a building plan that the congregation had talked about for years and done nothing about. After getting the go-ahead from the congregation, he rallied support from community leaders, and a building project was set in motion. By early 1954, the present sanctuary and annex of the El Buen Pastor Methodist Church in Santa Paula, with classrooms and a kitchen, had been built.

During 1955, I went to work for Johnson and Western Company, the company I had worked for in Temecula. They had a job in San Diego installing a storm drain that would run from the waterfront alongside of Lindberg Airport to the highway and along the railroad tracks to Washington Boulevard. I roomed with the project engineer in a rooming house on Sixth Street next to Balboa Park. It was a difficult project because we had to drill under the highway and push large sections of pipe two feet at a time. It was a tricky job, but we did it. I was responsible for installing the lateral pipes that connected to the main drain.

On one occasion, using a winch truck, we were to lay an eighteen-inch concrete pipe under an existing twelve-inch high-pressure gas line. Our plan was to lower the pipe over the gas line, then swing it to the side and then lower it again so it would fall under the gas main. As we lowered the pipe, the winch on the truck malfunctioned, and the pipe dropped right on top of the gas main and cracked it. The gas began to escape with a tremendous roar. I ran and stopped the traffic on the busy street while another person ran to call the gas company. What we didn't realize was that the escaping gas was going through the pipe already connected to the main storm drain. Inside the main storm drain, some two blocks away, were two elderly laborers patching the pipe joints between sections of pipe and using open-flame carbide lamps to see in the darkness. As the gas fumes reached them, one of the workers dropped down to the bottom of the pipe the moment he smelled the gas while the other man kept working. When the escaping gas got to his open-flame lamp, it ignited, and there was a tremendous explosion. The escaping gas from the gas line caught on fire, and flames shot up into the air, and an electrical pole nearby began to burn. A half block away was a fire station, and they saw what was happening, but did not react because no one called them until a few minutes later.

What I learned later that day was that the old man who had kept on working was fried alive. A brave truck driver who saw what had happened disregarded the tremendous heat inside the storm drain and ran in to check on the two men working inside. A few minutes later, he came out carrying the burnt old man who only had his belt on. Everything else was burnt off his body. He was rushed to the hospital where he died three days later. The other man who had dropped down on his belly came out with just moderate burns. That incident had a great impact on me. I couldn't understand why a machine we had used over and over would break during the most dangerous time. It was a tragedy long to be remembered. The project lasted nine months. I used to drive home to Santa Paula every weekend except when it was my turn to oversee the safety of our excavations during the weekend.

Right after that job, the company was the low bidder on a water pipeline system that was to be installed from La Mesa, north of San Diego, to Lakeside, a few miles northeast. I was the foreman in charge of the backfill operations of the project. Eventually, my family moved into a motel in El Cajon, east of San Diego. My son Johnnie Al started attending a school adjacent to the motel. My daughter, Patsy, as we used to call her, was growing up very quickly. The motel, which I paid by the week, was not the best but it was all I could afford. While there, we attended a Spanish Baptist church nearby. We liked the way the minister's son played the piano, which made for happy hymn singing. Living in El Cajon made it easy for us to visit the San Diego Zoo, the Museum of Natural History and the Art Museum. We also took boat rides around the bay and visited Tijuana. There was a time when Naomi became ill, and my mother came to stay with us to take care of the kids. The job there lasted nine months.

After the San Diego job, I was recommended to another big company, which was building a huge storm drain along Normandy Avenue in Gardena, California. I got the job which was to install lateral storm drain pipes into the box channel. The project superintendent was a man who had been a carpenters' superintendent when I worked at Matilija Dam north of Ojai years earlier. On my first day on the job, he told me, "You take care of your job, and I won't bother you, and don't ask for my help." I learned very quickly to work independently and to be self-reliant. I worked for five months on that project; and from there, I was again recommended for a job on San Nicolas Island, some sixty miles offshore from Point Mugu where we built a road and a baseball field for the navy. There were men from different crafts working for the navy on the small island. We all stayed in large barracks. On off hours, we would go around the island looking for good places to fish. The navy would fly us to the island on Monday mornings from Point Mugu and back on Fridays after work. Working on the island was not bad except when the wind blew. A strong wind would blow for two weeks at a time and then cease for a week or so. We had to wear scarves around our faces to ward off a sandblast.

When work ended a few months later, I went to work for a contractor who was placing rocks, or riprap as it is called, on the inner face of Casitas Dam just north of the City of Ventura. Operating a bulldozer, I pushed large rocks that had been dumped by trucks to a place where a crane would pick them up and then place them on the inner face of the dam. I remember that Senator Clair Engle, who was campaigning for reelection, came to ride the bulldozer with me so reporters could take his picture.

From the Casitas Dam job, I was sent to do the same kind of work at a power plant on the beach near the city of Oxnard where they were building a breakwater. After that, I worked for various construction firms on short jobs in the county and in the San Fernando Valley. That year, my son Johnnie Al joined the Boy Scouts and I got involved in the parents' committee of the troop, which was sponsored by our church.

In 1960, I once again went to work for David in the Valley. I worked for him all that year until he went broke which I assume was due to the mismanagement of his business. I had a tough time getting my checks cashed. In fact, when he paid us, we would all rush to the bank because we knew that the first to get there would get his check cashed. Although David had been so good to me, I finally quit the job at a loss of unpaid wages in the amount of $1,800 which at the time was a lot of money to me.

Albino, Naomi, Johnnie Al and Patsy　　　　*Albino 1954*

Johnnie Al and Patsy Pineda

Back row: nephews Jackie Vargas, Bobby Vargas, Sammy David Salas, daughter Patsy Pineda, son Johnnie Al Pineda, Sitting: nephews Morris Taylor Jr. and Harold James Kennedy

Dolls drawn by Patsy Pineda

Front Row: Harold James Kennedy, Jackie Vargas, Patsy Pineda, Bobby Vargas, Middle Row: Tita F. Vargas, Gary Kennedy, David Salas and Johnnie Al Pineda, Back Row: John G. Salas, Toni S. Kennedy, Naomi S. Pineda, Albino Pineda, Far back: Concepcion M. Salas

Patsy, Albino, Johnnie Al

Chapter XXII

BUYING OUR SECOND HOME

It was December 1960 when we bought the house I live in now. We bought it for $17,600. The house has four bedrooms, and two bathrooms. We gave two thousand dollars down and assumed a GI loan. We needed a room for each of our growing children, and this looked like a good house in a good neighborhood. Our son Johnnie Al was attending Isbell Junior High School, and Patsy was attending Blanchard. Our new home had plenty of rooms and a large backyard. I was fortunate that I was working for a landscaping company in the Valley and that my job lasted a couple of years. In 1961, our daughter joined the Girl Scouts, and Naomi got involved as a den mother. We wanted to expose our children to activities that would help them develop their character.

This was also the year my mother passed away. She suffered from high blood pressure and died of a stroke. She was seventy-three years old at the time. She had been living with my oldest half-sister, Lucy, who called me. I rushed to my mother's bedside and learned that there had been nothing her attending doctor could do for her. I remember kneeling by her bed and placing my face against hers, which was still warm. My thoughts went back to all the years that she suffered raising her children under the most trying of circumstances. When my father died, I was too young to understand the death of a loved one. But with my mother's death, I felt as if a part of my life had ceased to exist. My consolation came from the words of Christ as recorded in the Bible, which assure us that even though our bodies die, our souls will return to our creator for eternity. My mother was a very humble person who always tried to please those around her. She loved her grandchildren, especially those that were around her all the time. But it was her time to go, and the sadness was ours to bear.

During 1962, I struggled with seasonal employment but somehow, we were able to cope. We enjoyed seeing our children grow and fortunately, we were still able to provide for their needs as they attended school. Our former home, which we now rented out, provided some of the much-needed income for our household. We were happy in our new neighborhood although we noticed that families that had lived there for some time were selling their homes. I don't know whether they were selling because we were the first Mexican-American family to move into what was an all-white neighborhood or because most were elderly and wanted a smaller home to live in. We never knew why. The neighbors who had homes close to ours were very friendly and always cordial with us. Eventually, other Mexican-American families began to move into the neighborhood. We kept busy with our children participating with them in the different activities they were involved in. When we were not involved with Boy Scout activities with our son, we were involved in Girl Scout activities with our daughter.

The year 1963 was a year of blessings and healing. The first blessing was that the union called to offer me a job with a company from Fresno, California, that was installing a sewer pipeline in Montecito near Santa Barbara. I took it, and it turned out to be a good job. I started making good money.

Around this time, I still continued to be afflicted with asthma. One morning, I woke up, and the ceiling of our bedroom seemed to be going in circles. Vertigo was something I had never experienced before, so the doctor came to see me at my home and told me that he suspected that I had Ménière's disease. A few days later, I had another attack of vertigo while at work. I had to lie down in my car until I felt normal again and was able to finish the day's work. A week later, I had another attack as I was getting up in the morning. The doctor told me that I would have to have an operation in my ears, which would leave me completely deaf for the rest of my life. As I looked back for clues of what had triggered the vertigo, I recalled that I had been drinking frozen orange juice the night before the last two attacks, so I thought that perhaps I was allergic to frozen orange juice.

In desperation, Naomi called Mrs. Flores, who had been our neighbor on Oak Street and who was a devout Christian. She asked her if she could come and pray for me. My wife had a lot of faith in that woman's ability to pray. I recall that when my wife called Mrs. Flores, Mrs. Flores said, "Naomi, the only time you call me is when you need prayer. I'll be there in a while." She came with a man and prayed for me for about half an hour. She prayed fervently, almost demanding God to bring healing to me; and apparently, the Lord heard her prayer because soon after I went back to work.

After we finished the job in Santa Barbara, I went with the same company to northern California and worked there for two weeks in Concord, California. I noticed that the vertigo and asthma no longer bothered me. That was fifty-three years ago, and since then I haven't suffered from asthma or vertigo. I even drink frozen orange juice, which I thought was the culprit. That experience made me believe in the power of prayer, and I have come to believe that God responds not only to personal prayer but to intercessory prayer as well as in my case.

Towards the end of 1963, after working briefly for local companies, I was called back to work for the Fresno company I had worked for earlier. They had a new job in Oxnard, California, a twenty-minute drive from my home. Meanwhile, Naomi decided to get a job as well. She applied for and got a job with Montgomery Ward in their newly opened catalog store in the Santa Paula shopping center, which wass just a block away from our home. She worked with two other women in the store, and liked dealing with customers.

Then, in April 1964, Naomi discovered that she was pregnant. We were in our mid-life years but since we only had two children, a third child was welcome. The only thing was that the newborn would be thirteen years younger than our youngest child, Patsy. At our age, it was a little embarrassing to be expecting, yet we were very excited. Johnnie Al was in his senior year in high school, and Patsy was in junior high school. She was doing really well in school. That year, she received an award for a science fair project. We were always very proud of our children because they were conscientious about their responsibilities, both at home and at school. I remember Johnnie Al getting a job clearing weeds in a lemon orchard to earn some spending money.

Meanwhile, the company I was working for got a job at a Nevada Test Site, and I went to work with them in Nevada. The job consisted of installing a water pipeline along one of the roads. We lodged in government trailers, and since there were many other crafts working there, we all ate in a common mess hall. I used to come home every other weekend. My pastime at the site was to roam the nearby mountains in search of Indian arrowheads. In time, I had a small collection, which I brought home. After working there for about two months, I returned to the job in Oxnard, which was in the finishing stages. After that, I worked for other companies on short jobs.

My Mother - Dolores R. Pineda

Chapter XXIII

BIRTH OF OUR THIRD CHILD

Our third child, Paul, was born on December 30, 1964. I was working in the county and was finally able to be with Naomi as she gave birth to our last child. I was with her in the hospital until she began to deliver. At that point, the doctor told me to wait in the waiting room. About an hour later, the doctor came out and congratulated me for being the father of a newborn son who weighed eight pounds, six ounces. I went in to see how Naomi was doing and she asked, "Have you seen the baby?" I told her no. After being with her a while and seeing that she was all right, I told her that I was going to go see the baby. I went to the nursery where all the newborns were and as I looked through a large window, a nurse pointed to my son who was yawning as if it were time to go to sleep. I was elated knowing that mother and child were doing all right. I then called my two children at home and told them that baby Paul had arrived. They had been eagerly awaiting my call and were very excited about their new baby brother. When baby Paul was brought home, he became the family's center of attention and remained so for many years.

After giving birth, Naomi went back to work but soon Montgomery Ward closed the catalog store. Naomi decided to stay home to take care of the baby. I continued to work sporadically in the area and was heavily involved in our church as chair of the official board, chair of the Christian Education Commission, and chair of the Boy Scouts Parent Committee. That year, Johnnie Al joined a Boy Scout Explorer's Post, which I got involved with as well. Earlier in the year, Johnnie Al and Patsy had been baptized and became members of our church, El Buen Pastor United Methodist Church.

The year 1965 started well, but soon, it brought sadness to my life with the death of my youngest brother Isidro or "Sid" as he was called, who died on April 16 of an asthma attack in a doctor's office. He was only thirty-seven years old. I loved Sid, who held a special place in my heart because he was the baby of the family. I was always very protective of him, but for some reason, as he grew older and joined the army, he began to distance himself from me. After he was discharged from the army, he married an Anglo woman, and they had two children—Frankie and Albena. After a while, they divorced, and she left Santa Paula. I never saw Frankie or Albena again. Then, later on, Sid married another Anglo woman who bore him two sons. Unfortunately, after his death, his widow and the two boys got into trouble with the law and as of this writing, I don't know of their whereabouts.

That same year, I was called by my former employer company from Fresno to go to work for them in Redding, California, where they were going to install a large system of water lines from the Sacramento River to the eastern outlying areas. I went to Redding and found lodging at the home of a couple who would provide room and board. I shared a small room with the woman's ninety-year-old father. The house was in a neighborhood just across the river, about half a mile from downtown Redding. The old man always made sure that I paid the weekly rent before I left for the weekend. I used to come home on weekends. I would take the Greyhound bus at 6:00 p.m. on Friday after work and travel all night. I would arrive in Castaic around 8:00 a.m. on Saturday morning where Naomi and baby Paul would be waiting for me. On Sunday evening, I would again board the bus at Castaic and arrive in Redding on Monday morning at 6:00 a.m. I would then walk the half mile to the boarding house, get my truck, and head for work. Mondays were always a long day for me for obvious reasons.

Redding, like other cities, had some strange characters. One early morning, I arrived at the bus station and as I was going out the door carrying my suitcase, a young man standing by the door greeted me by saying, "Good morning! Beautiful morning, isn't it?"

It was still dark, but I said, "Yes it is," and kept on going. From the bus terminal, halfway to the river bridge, I had to walk along a dark street before turning one block to the main highway that crossed the river. As I was walking that morning, I sensed that someone was following me and as I looked back, I saw a figure dash behind a parked car. I knew it was the guy who had greeted me at the bus station door. Annoyed, I was tempted to go back and ask him what he was up to but instead, I turned the corner and walked to the main highway. As I was approaching the bridge, he came up in front of me from the next side street and asked me if I was heading up north. He said that he was driving in that direction and wanted someone to ride with him for company. I told him that I was just going across the bridge to where I lived. He then turned around and went back to town. A couple of weeks later, I saw him again at the bus terminal, and I almost stopped to ask him if he was still waiting for someone to ride with him up north. Instead, I kept on walking. I never figured out what he really had in mind.

I found Redding an interesting and beautiful town with a river and lakes nearby. It had a forest with pine trees and streams where one could fish. The man where I boarded was an avid fisherman. We often had fresh grilled trout for dinner.

One reason I came home every weekend was because I wanted to be with my family, and I wanted baby Paul to feel that he had a father. The other reason was that I was teaching a youth Sunday school class on Sunday mornings. I had committed myself to Christ and to his church.

During the summer of that year, my family came to stay with me. I remember driving up north through the Sacramento Valley. The temperature was in the hundreds, and my car didn't have air-conditioning. It was so hot that we kept placing wet towels on our baby's head to keep him cool. But just the thought of the family being together made up for all the discomfort. We rented a motel outside of Redding, and on the weekends, we would drive to the nearby lakes where we would go swimming. On other occasions, we would drive to the forest. Having the family with me was a delight. My son Johnnie Al had graduated from high school that year and was ready to attend Ventura Junior College.

I worked in Redding from April to November 1965. From there, the company got a short job in between Jackson and Ione, California, installing a gas line in quaint mining towns. I found lodging in a motel in the town of

Lodi where I stayed without my family. Winter was setting in, and Naomi and baby Paul came in a Greyhound bus to spend a weekend with me. Later on, I got Johnnie Al a job with the company while he was on winter break. At the end of the job, we both drove back home. Johnnie Al was very appreciative of the job superintendent for letting him work for a couple of weeks. In fact, he sent him a card expressing his thanks for the opportunity to work for the company—a nice gesture by my son.

My Brother - Ysidro R. Pineda

Joe Marquez with baby Paul Pineda in his arms

Chapter XXIV

GOOD JOBS AND COMMUNITY INVOLVEMENT

As the year 1966 started, I was home working on and off as usual until the month of April when the union dispatched me to work for a large company that was building a section of Ridge Route freeway near Gorman. I went to work for them on the swing shift, from 4:30p.m. to 11:00 p.m.and would carpool with other operators from the area. I started operating a D9 bulldozer and later a motor blade. The company then assigned me to run a Quad 9 push cat, which consisted of two D9 tractors hooked in tandem. I operated both tractors from the front one. Quad 9s were used to push earthmovers (scrapers) as they loaded the dirt. To me, running two machines meant better pay. Different kinds of heavy equipment were used on the project day and night. Working at night was very dangerous because of the steep terrain, yet I enjoyed it because I always liked working with bulldozers, especially when I was sent to do pioneering work. I was the first to break the paths on hillsides so the rest of the equipment could start carving the mountains for the roadways. I felt good because I finally had a job that would last for a while. Running two machines made for a good weekly paycheck. And, I would return home at the end of every day.

That year, our son Johnnie Al made us very proud for becoming the first scout of our church sponsored Boy Scout Troop 307 to reach the rank of Eagle Scout. Prior to that, he received the God and Country Award. Our son loved the outdoors, and being a Boy Scout was just the perfect activity for him. Johnnie Al also joined the Order of the Arrow and during one of his outings, he designed a shoulder patch for the scouts. Little did he know that his activities as a Boy Scout would eventually help him develop into a fine army intelligence officer. I will elaborate more on that later.

Also that year, as chair of the Pastor/Parish Relations Committee of my church, I suggested that we end our financial dependency on the church conference which was paying for our pastors. The committee approved my recommendation and we have been a self-supporting church ever since.

My job in Gorman continued to provide a good weekly paycheck. Winters on the job were tough with temperatures dropping twenty degrees below zero at night. We all wore warm clothing but were still cold. Sometimes, we would reverse the radiator fans of the tractors so the engine heat would blow towards us, but in addition to the heat came a dust with a sandblasting force. We had to wear goggles, scarves, and dust masks for protection. Nonetheless, we survived the winter of 1966.

In the year 1967, Johnnie Al, who now preferred to be called John, was accepted at University of California at Santa Barbara and Patsy, who also preferred to be called Patricia, was chosen to go with a group of girls from the high school on a tour of several countries in Europe. Like our oldest son, little did Patricia know that someday, she would be a world traveler which I will discuss later. Our youngest child, Paul, was growing up and he was the center of attention especially with his sister who took him wherever she went including on dates.

That same year, we bought a small rental house for $8,500, which in later years would prove to be a good investment. As 1968 rolled around, my job in Gorman came to an end. It ended early in the spring and some of us were transferred to the Castaic Dam project, which was being built by the same contractor. After two weeks, they decided that they didn't need us after all and that was the end of one of my best jobs. Those of us who were laid off went to claim unemployment benefits, something I had been accustomed to doing.

That spring, I took Naomi and Paul to see the "desert flowers." We drove to Escondido and then up the mountains through Julian and Ramona, to Borrego Springs, and then on to Palm Springs. The temperature was already in the hundreds, so we decided to take the tram up to San Jacinto Peak. When we got to the top, there was snow on the ground, and it was freezing. We didn't stay long because we hadn't brought jackets. It was a learning experience.

Back home, for the rest of the year, I worked on and off—no steady jobs. I also became more involved in the community. A new interest of mine was getting involved in the newly organized Title VII Bilingual Education Advisory Committee which served the local elementary school district. I served six years on that committee and three as the chairman. I recall going through some very difficult times during those years. Many people were against bilingual education, especially when the school district employed a controversial person as director. School board meetings were always packed with upset people.

At home, Naomi wasn't feeling well physically. During the fall, she had experienced a hemorrhage, and I had to rush her to the hospital. Our doctor decided that she needed to have a hysterectomy, so she underwent surgery. After that, she never felt well again. She always complained of being exhausted. Her health was also challenged by her diabetes. She nevertheless tried to enjoy life as much as she could.

Throughout our marriage, we were church-going people—always involved in the life of the church. Naomi had learned a lot about money from the experience of working in her family's grocery store. She was a penny-pincher because she knew that money did not come easily and she wanted to make sure that we always had a rainy day fund. I always turned my paychecks over to her because I knew she had the ability to handle our finances effectively. Our bills were always paid on time.

In December of that same year, I went to work nights again for a contractor who was grading residential lots and digging two large excavations for what is now Westlake Village near Thousand Oaks. I worked there for about three months bringing home good paychecks.

When the year 1969 started, I continued to work in the area, and I became heavily involved in the community. In addition to my involvement with the schools, I was persuaded to enter the local political scene by running for a seat on the high school board of trustees. I knew little about politics, but with the support and encouragement of many individuals, I braved the challenge. I learned to run a good campaign, but even so, I lost by fifty votes. The campaign for the high school board seat was an eye-opener for me. There were two long-time members of the board who had served for several years. They had decided that they had served their terms and were not interested in seeking re-election. However, when they got wind that two Hispanics (one of whom was me) were running for the board, they immediately changed their minds. They apparently thought Hispanics were not qualified to serve the community in positions of importance. As it turned out, the other Mexican-American, a businessman,was elected, which helped break down the barriers of prejudice. Shortly after my defeat, during one of the high school PTA meetings, I was elected vice-chair of the group. I was also invited to join a group of citizens known as Concerned Parents for Education.

*Older Brother -
Manuel R. Pineda*

*Family: Front - Paul, Sitting -
Naomi, Albino, Standing -
Johnnie Al and Patsy*

Chapter XXV

THE EARLY 1970s

The year of 1970 continued to be a time of interesting events. First, Naomi became treasurer of our church for the second time. Little Paul got a dog he named Happy. Our son John, who was attending the University of California at Santa Barbara, went through the experience of the Isla Vista riots. In fact, he was involved in the sense that when a fire was started in a trash bin behind the Bank of America, he didn't think it was right so he jumped in and put the fire out. After that act, he began to get vicious and threatening letters. He couldn't believe the hatred he drew from his act. Nevertheless, he stood strong in defense of what he had done and what he believed. He continued with his studies and had a part-time job drawing cartoons for the *Goleta Valley Sun*. He was an art major and drawing cartoons was something he did well. He also had a part-time job working for Montgomery Ward in Ventura. John graduated from UCSB in 1971 and then attended University of Southern California for one year where he studied urban planning.

Patricia, on the other hand, graduated from high school in 1970 and was accepted to Mills College in Oakland, California. Mills is a small, private women's college. Patricia, like John, was very self-reliant in the sense that while attending school, she always found a job somewhere to help support herself. While in high school, she had worked for a hamburger place at the east end of town called Terry's and then for Foster's Freeze. The owner of Foster's Freeze, Mr. Thor, had been a neighbor and was always good to Patricia. He always wanted her to work and Patricia enjoyed the job of flipping burgers and making shakes.

Meanwhile, at home, Naomi continued to be the great administrator of our household. In 1971, we were able to buy another rental property. Our son Paul was enrolled in kindergarten at Glen City School, a few blocks from our home. Patricia was in Mexico attending the University of Puebla. She was studying under the Mills College Junior Year Abroad Program. That year, I was sent by the school district to a bilingual seminar in San Diego, which was held at the El Cortez Hotel. School representatives from all over the Western region attended.

John, in the meantime, ran out of deferrals and joined the army under the Delayed Entry Program. Before reporting to Fort Ord, he went on a trip to Mexico in search of relatives from his mother's side. As I mentioned earlier, he had worked part-time for Montgomery Ward in their garden center in Ventura and with the money he earned, he bought a snazzy Datsun sports car, which he drove to Mexico. His trip inspired other cousins to do the same in years that followed.

Chapter XXVI

THE SANTA BARBARA ROMERO CANYON FOREST FIRE

The Romero Canyon forest fire took place in Santa Barbara, California during the Fall of 1971. I was working at the Rocklite Plant site in Ventura running a D8 bulldozer. My job consisted of carving the mountainside behind the plant site on North Ventura Avenue. After carving out clay from the mountainside, I pushed it down the mountainside to a place where it was picked up by a skip loader and dumped into a crusher. A conveyor would then run the crushed clay into hot ovens. The end product that came out of the ovens was a light rock used to decorate gardens and roadways.

One day, my boss came over to tell me that I had to go help fight the forest fire in Santa Barbara using the bulldozer. The bulldozer was loaded onto a low-bed hauler and I followed the hauler up to the top of the San Marcos Pass, which is located north of Santa Barbara. We turned onto Camino Del Cielo, which runs along the top of the mountain range facing the city.

When we got to the unloading place, I remember all the commotion that was going on as my tractor was being unloaded. It reminded me of a battlefront during the war. Different kinds of equipment and fire trucks were coming and going. As I waited for instructions, I heard over one of the fire truck's loud speakers that a tractor operator and three other men had been killed by the fire down below the mountain. It made me nervous but lucky for me, I was on top of the mountains where, at that time, it was safer. As I looked down the mountain, I saw one of the most spectacular views I had ever seen. Entire orchards were engulfed in flames all along the foot of the mountain. A prayer came to my lips, "God help those working down below."

I was instructed to clear fire trails where the fire had not yet burned. Even though I had a forest department man guiding me, it was still very dangerous work. The terrain was very rocky, and tractors have a tendency to slide very easily when running on rocky surfaces. On one occasion, my guide directed me to clear a path along a steep ridge and as I began to push a pile of brush in front of my tractor, the big pile of brush suddenly disappeared. I stopped and walked over on top of the hood of the tractor to look, and discovered that I had stopped at the very edge of a three-hundred-foot cliff. I worked straight through from the previous day to the next morning. In the morning, a helicopter came and took me to a rest camp down below, which had been set up in a football field in Montecito. There were army cots everywhere, and there was a huge kitchen where they served enormous steaks three times a day. They also had huge water troughs filled with ice and fruit juices. We were also given box lunches to take with us. They consisted of a beef sandwich, a large cookie, a candy bar, and a can of fruit juice. I was to sleep during the day and work a twelve-hour shift during the night.

During this forest fire experience, I noticed how much food was allowed to go to waste. One early morning as I went from one ridge to another, I came upon a pile of lunch boxes as big as a car. Someone had just dumped them there and I remember stopping to get a sack full of cookies, candy, and cans of juice.

After my first two nights there, my job was to build a road along the top of the mountains. The forest department felt that a road was necessary, which was right. Working at night, where the brush and grass had burned, was very dangerous because the ground was black and you couldn't see whether you were near a ledge. In addition, the wind would blow at night, which made it very difficult to see what one was doing. Nevertheless, I was able to finish the road I was assigned to build. Later, I learned that my employer had received a certificate of merit from the forest department for a job well done under trying circumstances. I felt good about that. I worked in the fire area for about two weeks until the fire was finally put out. In my mind, I can still hear the howling of coyotes.

After that experience, I was given some time off from work but eventually went back to work at the hillside job in Ventura. The job was not too steady, but it was interesting. As I dug around ninety feet into the mountain, I pulled out huge seashells. One time, I dug out a limb from a pine tree, which had a pinecone at one end in perfect condition and an oily substance at the other end. That meant that thousands of years ago, there were pine trees in what was now a bare mountain. Also, the presence of the seashells indicated that at one time, the sea was as high as the mountain.

Chapter XXVII

CONTINUATION OF THE 70s

During 1972, we experienced some rioting in our community, and people got together to form a community council to deal with the tension left behind from the rioting. The council was formed, and I ended up being the chair. Our police chief was the vice-chair and two other citizens joined the committee. We met a few times and heard complaints, mostly from activists. In time, things cooled down, and the council was disbanded. That year, I also went to a bilingual education conference in Austin, Texas, representing our school district.

In January of 1973, Naomi, Paul, and I drove to Mexico. We drove in our new Audi, which was the second Audi sold in the county. Our destination was Puebla,Mexico where our daughter, Patricia, was studying at the Universidad De Las Americas under the Mills College Junior Year Abroad Program. On our way, we stopped in the city of Torreón where Naomi had uncles, aunts, and other relatives. One night, we took Naomi's cousin and his wife, who were our hosts, out to dinner. They wanted Naomi to taste the steak that was served at the restaurant so they ordered a huge steak for her. Just looking at the huge meal made Naomi sick. Her blood pressure went up and a doctor had to be summoned.

After staying in Torreon for a couple of days, a bank employee known to the family offered to drive us in our car to Mexico City since he knew the way to our destination and happened to be going in that direction for a business trip. He drove us to Mexico City and got us a hotel. I was afraid to drive in Mexico's traffic, but the following day, we ventured out and drove to the Teotihuacán pyramids.

A couple of days later, we took off for Puebla to visit Patricia. Our daughter actually lived in Cholula, a small village outside of Puebla, near the University of the Americas where she was studying. Patricia lived in a house she had rented with a girl who came from a respected Santa Paula family. They had been best of friends in high school and were now studying at the same university in Mexico. The girl was Louise Folks. After visiting with them, we had the opportunity to go to the city of Puebla where we enjoyed a nice dinner. From Patricia's house, one could see the twin snow-capped volcanoes named Popocatépetl and Iztaccihuatl. After spending a couple of days in Puebla and Cholula, we returned to Mexico City. Patricia and Louise came with us to Mexico City where we attended a ballet at the Palacio de Bellas Artes. Paul and I went up to the tower of the Pan-American building to take in a view of the city. We all went to Chapultepec Park and also visited the Museo Nacional de Artes and the Museo Nacional de Antropologia. Just as we were going into the latter, Naomi almost passed out on us. She had become ill due to the altitude, so we had to leave.

A couple of days later, Patricia and Louise left for Cholula on a bus as we left for home. I drove to Queretaro then to Celaya on our way to Irapuato where we stayed for the night. The next day, we left for Aguas Calientes where we planned to stop to visit a relative of my mother-in-law's. His name was Federico Martinez. When we got to the outskirts of the city, I stopped to look at a map. As I did, two young men in a car stopped and offered to take us to the address we were looking for. We followed them, and they took us right to Federico's house. Good deed! We visited with Federico's family and enjoyed lunch together. We gave them some canned puddings, which they loved.

After our visit with Federico and his family, we continued on our way back. We stopped and spent the night in Zacatecas and then drove onto Torreón where we also stayed one night. Then, we took off for El Paso, Texas. On the way, we stopped in the city of Chihuahua and visited the estate of Pancho Villa. We visited Mrs. Villa and then left for El Paso. Our son John was at Fort Bliss at the time, so we visited him. The next day, we headed for home. It was the first long trip that Naomi had ever taken. It was a great experience because we had never been to Mexico City before.

Our son John, who had completed basic training the year before, had applied for and been accepted into the Army Military Intelligence with some assistance from our congressman. After taking counter intelligence and Vietnamese language courses, he was assigned to Taegu, Korea, with the rank of special agent. He remained in Korea until 1975.

All this time, I continued to work for different companies. The jobs were short-lived but good paying. That same year, I became involved as a board member of what was known as Welcome Home for delinquent boys. We rented a house on the main street near downtown and employed a director to supervise the home. That program lasted until 1978. We had problems with the director, and the home was shut down. It was during that year that we enrolled Paul in the Cub Scouts. However, he chose not to follow in his brother footsteps.

In the area of my church involvement, we were in the process of forming a construction committee, which would help raise funds for the demolition of the parsonage building next to the church. Our plan was to build an educational wing adjacent to the existing church buildings. I never dreamed that I would be so involved in so many meetings and activities. It felt good to be able to make so many contributions to my church and the community.

The year 1974 was a year of significant events. First, our daughter, Patricia, graduated from Mills College. Her graduation was an important event for her and for us. She also had been in an accident and broke her pelvis so on graduation day she had to walk with crutches. She was a very determined girl. We never had to push her. When she wanted something, she went after it. She always searched for her own scholarships and was very fortunate to get them.

Patricia developed a strong personality while in college. Although she and her mother were always very close, they got into arguments. I would come home, and Naomi would be weeping; and right away, I knew that she and Patricia had argued. This happened many times, but Patricia would always call later to make up with her mother. John, on the other hand, was a very easy-going and non-combative young man.

Naomi's life was her husband and her children. She loved them dearly. I remember one time when Patricia, with a smile on her face, asked me, "Dad, which of your children do you love the best?" My answer was, "I love John the best because he is our firstborn, and I love you the best because you are our only daughter. I also love Paul the best because he is our youngest child." She said, "I get what you mean."

The second significant event was that Patricia applied for and was accepted at Boalt Hall School of Law at the University of California at Berkeley. She was shaping the future of her life in a way that neither she nor we had quite anticipated. Our prayers were simply that she would maximize her God-given talents and live a happy, productive life. We wanted our children to get the education we didn't have, and to grow to become successful in life without forgetting the Christian upbringing they had all received.

The third significant event that year was the resignation of President Nixon. I, as a life-long Democrat, for the first and only time, had voted for a Republican when I voted for Nixon. One of the reasons I voted for Nixon was that was he was a native Californian although he turned out to be a great disappointment. I felt sorry for the man. I remember seeing him at Disneyland and asking him for his autograph. He took the time to give it to me and to my children.

At this point of my life, I enjoyed good health, and my energy level was pretty high. In addition to caring for my family, I was engaged in church and community activities that were extremely rewarding. I was fortunate that the union was dispatching me to jobs that were within close driving distance, which allowed me to stay active in both the church and community.

Chapter XXVIII

MY ELECTION TO PUBLIC OFFICE

The year of 1975 was very eventful. Since I had a child in elementary school, I decided, with the encouragement of many people, to run for election to the school board. I began to test the waters by talking to those who had helped other candidates in the past. All encouraged me to run. I took out the papers and began my campaign. I received the support of many people who campaigned for me and I walked the city from house to house. I attended many forums, and learned a lot about politics. Some things I liked and some things I hated about politics. In the end, all my work and the support of others paid off. On March 4, I won a seat on the Elementary School District Board of Trustees. When I read the local paper the next day, I discovered that I had been the major vote getter in all the city's precincts. What a thrill! Never in my wildest dreams had I ever thought I would be an elected official. On the day of my first meeting, I was the most nervous person in town.

At first, I had trouble understanding some of the terms that were used in the schools such as COLA. To me COLA meant "tail" in Spanish, but after asking many questions, I came to understand many things, including that COLA means cost-of-living adjustment. I still had a lot to learn, but then I realized that everything I knew was learned the hard way. Sitting in front of an audience concerned about their own individual interests who expected the board to address those interests was something to reckon with. When I ran for the board, I had no axes to grind. All I wanted was to be a member of that decision-making body and to be able to contribute my ideas so that the children attending our local

160

schools would receive the best education possible. The proper selection of teachers and other personnel had much to do with the quality of education we were to provide. Funding from the state was always inadequate, and the issue of teacher and personnel demands for salary increases was forever before us.

There were times when I would come to the board meetings, which were held at city hall, and would find a crowd of teachers with posters and signs waiting for the meeting to start. I would arrive and walk among them reading the individual posters and signs. I sympathized with their concerns around salaries, but the budget presented to us would not allow much for salary increases. Santa Paula was and still is a low tax base community.

I remember one time when I read a sign that had been written by a Spanish teacher. The sign had the sentence No Sean Agarados, which was misspelled. It should have been said No Sean Agarrados. When the meeting started, I felt tempted to say, "How can we consider dealing with the issue of salary increases when you can't even spell a picket sign correctly?" But, of course, I knew it would be inappropriate to say anything and I would never have wanted to cause anyone unnecessary embarrassment or humiliation. In particular, I didn't want to embarrass the teacher who had written the sign. Maintaining good relations with the teaching staff and other personnel was very important to me as a school board member.

I do recall one meeting when a teacher who was speaking for the teachers' union said, "Since we are not getting a raise, I told my fellow teachers not to do their best in their classrooms." Hearing that statement, I could not restrain myself to remain silent. As chair of the board I told him, "You just made me lose respect for you as a schoolteacher. I wish I had never heard that statement." I meant every word. He didn't like what I told him, but I felt that it had to be said.

One of the hardest experiences of being the chair of the school board or being just a board member was dealing with unruly members of the public. In a hall jammed with people, it was difficult to single out the unruly ones. It took a great deal of patience to effectively manage such situations. I was considered a level-headed person by many people, and tried to remain so.

I was elected vice-chair of the school board of trustees three years in succession and three years as chair. I really enjoyed being a board member. Every year, I would attend a California School Boards Association annual conference which was typically held in San Francisco where we would attend a variety of workshops that had to do with school administration. I also would attend other workshop that became available because I wanted to learn all I could about schools. My election to the Ventura County School Boards Association was another involvement, which provided me with a great deal of experience. I served one year as secretary of that board, two years as second vice president, two years as first vice president, and two years as president. I was also elected to two two-year terms as a delegate to the California School Boards delegate assembly. I served a total of eight and a half years on the Santa Paula Elementary School board. On my third attempt for reelection, I lost by a small margin. Several board members wanted to get rid of the school superintendent, which was an action I didn't support. They campaigned hard to bring in two new members onto the board and succeeded. Eventually, the superintendent was fired at a high cost to the school district.

I remember that some two years before I left the board, a woman had written a letter to me complaining that some board members were getting a monthly stipend, and she thought that being a school board member should be a service to the community without compensation. Two of us never accepted any compensation (being on the board) other than reimbursement for our expenses when we went to conferences or workshops to represent the school district. It so happens that the same woman ran for the school board and got elected. I remember the first meeting she attended—she pulled me to one side and asked me in a whisper, "How much do board members get paid a month?" I couldn't believe what I was hearing. Here was the same woman who had chastised certain board members for getting a monthly stipend. My response to her was, "Some board members get a monthly stipend, but two of us have chosen not to receive anything other than a refund for expenses, and that is by choice."

My other area of involvement, which provided me with a great deal of experience, was serving on the Ventura County School Boards Redistricting Committee for nineteen years, with nine as president.

Santa Paula Elementary School District Members,
Center - Board Chair Albino R. Pineda

Chapter XXIX

THE SECOND HALF OF THE 1970s

The year of 1975 was the year my son John returned from South Korea with all kinds of commendations from the Korean government. John inherited his mother's personality and made friends easily. He was then reassigned to the Homestead Air Force Base military intelligence office in Florida.

That same year, our daughter, Patricia, who was still studying law at Berkeley, married a fellow law student who was of Jewish descent. They got married at Ojai United Methodist Church with all of our family and relatives in attendance as well as the groom's parents, brothers, and sister who came from San Francisco. Being of the Jewish faith, the parents were not too happy that their son was getting married in a Protestant church. But nevertheless, they were very cordial and after the ceremony, invited the wedding party and my family to a dinner at the Pierpont Inn in Ventura.

Our new son-in-law's name was Lewis Soffer. His father, Joseph, was a physician in San Francisco. He played the trumpet with a group of friends who gathered every week at Pier 39 in San Francisco (a beer joint) to play Dixieland jazz just for fun. On one occasion, we happened to be in San Francisco, so we went to Pier 39 to hear Joe and his friends play. During one of the numbers, Dr. Soffer or Joe turned to me and said, "Al, this is for you." And they began playing, "Just a little walk with thee, grant it, Jesus, is my plea."

That same year, our youngest son, Paul, won the fifth-grade fifty-yard dash and other races. My oldest half sister, Lucy, became a member of our church while I went to work for a well-known construction company that was installing a pipeline in Paso Robles. The job lasted about two months, and it was a good-paying job.

In 1976, I was invited to many events and was introduced to many important people. That year, I met Senator Alan Cranston at a barbecue. He was introduced to me by Mrs. Jane Tolmach who was a former Oxnard City mayor. Mrs. Tolmach was now running for the Thirty-sixth District seat in the state assembly. On another occasion, she introduced me to Los Angeles City Mayor Tom Bradley, who had come to Ventura to campaign for her. I also met the former Governor Edmund "Pat" Brown at Mrs. Tolmach's home and his son, Governor Jerry Brown.

That summer, Naomi, Paul, and I spent a week's vacation in Yosemite National Park, which we enjoyed very much. Patricia, who was still attending law school, got a summer job as a clerk at an Oxnard law firm. Also, I came home from work one day and Naomi surprised me by telling me that she had applied for a job as an instructional aide for the high school migrant program. She was always trying to be a provider as well. A few days later, she was informed that she had gotten the job. Naomi's personality and concern for young people blended well with the needs of the high school kids. She had that motherly counseling spirit, which the students appreciated and respected. Years later when they met her in the streets, they would hug her for all the help she had given them. We would attend the migrant program meetings and meet with the parents. Part of Naomi's job, besides being in the classroom, was to visit the parents at their homes. She loved her work.

Patricia graduated from law school the following year in 1977, and right after, she passed the bar and went to work as a deputy state public defender in San Francisco. John, meanwhile, got married to Mary Sawyer who was also in the army. She was a girl from Massachusetts. They were married in a military ceremony in Maryland. Naomi and I were unable to attend the wedding. Shortly after, John was sent to Monterey, California to study German for a year before being assigned to Giessen, Germany.

Meanwhile, at home, I went to work for a plumbing company that was installing plumbing in the building foundations of a Thousand Oaks mall. I operated a backhoe, digging the trenches for the plumbing pipes.

Patricia Salas Pineda

Warrant Officer - John A. Pineda and Mary Sawyer Wedding

Albino wih son Paul

Chapter XXX

MY LAST AND BEST JOB
BEFORE RETIREMENT

On July 12, 1978, I was dispatched by the union hall to a job with JFJ Engineering Construction Company in Camarillo. Judging from past experiences with local companies, I went to work for them expecting the job to last only from a few days to a few weeks. As it turned out, they liked my work and kept me busy. They also succeeded in getting job after job. New housing projects were sprouting all over, and we kept building storm drains. Soon, they bought a large Koering backhoe, and asked me to practice until I got the hang of how to operate the machine. It didn't take me long, and from then on, it was my machine to run. I would often work six days a week and began to earn good money. The owners were two brothers.

Once, we were working in Ventura, and I was picking up pipes with a large loader. As I scooped the pipes into the loader bucket, some of the ends of the pipes would chip because the pipes were very brittle. When the boss running the job (one of the brothers) saw the chipped pipe, he came to me and said, "I don't like the way you are chipping the pipes. You need to be more careful." Later on, I guess, he realized that moving pipes around with a loader without a helper wasn't easy; so at quitting time, he came over and said, "Good job," and handed me fifty dollars in cash. I guess he didn't want me to feel offended by his scolding behavior. From then on, both brothers were really good to me. As time went on, they discovered that I was an experienced operator and always did my work as if the company belonged to me. One time, they assigned me to excavate a deep trench in solid rock which is a very difficult task. Afterwards, one of the owners came over to look at the trench I had dug. He stopped me and climbed on the machine and said, "The trench looks good." He put his hand on mine and placed a hundred-dollar bill in my hand and said, "Take your wife out to dinner on me."

Working for Frank (who was the majority owner of the company) and Jack was a pleasant job. On another occasion, I was working in the Thousand Oaks area where I was running the big backhoe. The digging was easy, so I dug more trenches than had been expected for that day. Frank came over and said he was very pleased with the way the job was going, and said, "Take your wife out to dinner tonight," as he handed me a hundred-dollar bill. I suppose those were gestures of encouragement to keep doing a good job although I really didn't need tips for doing a good job. When I went to work for somebody, I always tried to do my very best. On Christmas Day, Frank would invite all the workers to have lunch at a pizza place, and would hand over envelopes with a cash bonus for each employee.

In 1979, my daughter, Patricia, left her state public defender's job and went to work for an Oakland law firm. That same year, she, Lewis, Naomi, our son Paul, and my sister-in-law Stella went on a vacation to Club Med in the southern part of Mexico. After they returned, Paul went to Germany to spend the rest of his summer vacation with his brother John who was then stationed in Germany. While there, John got Paul a job as stock clerk at the Giessen Post Exchange. He also had the opportunity to travel to Frankfurt, the Iron Curtain, Dachau, the Rhine Valley, Neuschwanstein Castle, Switzerland, the Alps, Austria, and Northern Italy. But when he returned from Europe, he complained that John had been too bossy. He was glad to be home. He returned just in time to begin the practice season with the Santa Paula High School's varsity football team.

The following year, 1980, turned out to be another eventful year. Patricia decided to go into corporate law and got a job with Itel Corporation based in San Francisco where she became senior counsel for the corporation. Her office was on the 24th floor of 2 Embarcadero Center which faces the Bay.

That same year, I began to teach a young adult Sunday school class at our church. During the summer, Richard Sawyer, Mary's brother who was serving in the navy, came to visit us and stayed for a few days. We showed him the area and took him to Santa Barbara and Solvang before he left.

The following year, 1981, turned out to be another eventful year. First, Mary gave birth to our first grandchild in Frankfurt, Germany. They named the baby boy, Jonathan Matteo Pineda.

Second, Patricia was appointed to the historically male-dominated Oakland Port Commission as the first female appointee where she served eight years (one year as chair of the board). On the day she was appointed, a great celebration sponsored by a number of Hispanic organizations from the Bay Area took place. The Mayor of Oakland, Lionel J. Wilson also received a threat on his life for not appointing an African-American woman.

While at Itel, Pat went to Mexico City to do negotiations with Ferrocarriles Nacionales de Mexico. Also, as a port commissioner, she and other commissioners traveled to many places, including South America. On other occasions, she went to Australia, Denmark, the Philippines, Thailand, Taiwan, China and Japan. She also went on a trip to Hong Kong, and South Korea to visit the Port of Incheon. She took our son, Paul, with her on that trip.

During the fiftieth anniversary celebration of the Golden Gate Bridge, Naomi and I accompanied Pat as the Oakland port commissioners celebrated the occasion aboard a large boat on the Bay with an orchestra. We had dinner on board and watched fireworks. Before that year was over, Patricia had filed for divorce from her husband Lewis Soffer. Like Patricia, he had passed the bar on his first try and had become a successful real estate lawyer but for some reason, their marriage did not work out although they remained good friends.

Naomi and I were frequent visitors to the Bay Area. During this particular year, we enjoyed a short vacation in Monterey,California where we dined at Cannery Row and visited some of the historic buildings of the area. At home, Paul (who was now in high school) was turning out to be an excellent football player. But on December of that year, during one of the home games, he ended up with a broken shoulder. We took him to the hospital where he had an operation, which ended his football career. After the operation, his comment was, "I'd rather eat a couple of Big Macs than hospital food." He was a big kid with a big appetite.

The year of 1982 found me campaigning for Gary Hart who was seeking the state assembly seat for our district. He was elected and served a few years and then he ran for the state senatorial seat for our district, which he also won. He served as a California state senator for some years before leaving the political arena.

That year, Naomi and I were pleasantly surprised when our daughter's name appeared on the Outstanding Young Women of America list. Our children were getting honors beyond our expectations.

During her college years, Patricia acquired a purebred German shepherd who became a huge lovable pet and companion for our smaller dog named Happy. The big dog was named Zapata. We all loved him. In the last two years of his life, we noticed that he was suffering from arthritis in his hind legs. One Friday night, he was scratching at the rear door of the house as if he was trying to tell us something. I went out while he stood there staring at me. As usual, I massaged his head with my hand and then went back into the house. On Sunday, we went to church, and Paul stayed home. During the service, I was told that there was a call for me on the phone. I picked up the phone, and heard Paul crying and saying, "Zapata is dead." I hung up, got in my car, and went home. Paul was crying, I hugged him, and we went outside. Zapata was lying on his belly just outside the doghouse with his legs spread out. We all cried that day. We loved that dog.

That year, Jack O'Connell started his campaign for the state assembly, and we met in a private home. He asked for our support, so we campaigned for him. He was elected to the state assembly.

The year of 1983 brought us happy as well as sad events. On the happy side, Paul graduated from high school but on the sad side, my eighty-one-year-old uncle, Joe, was hit and killed by an automobile while he crossed a street a block away from his house on Eighth Street. He had moved from Los Angeles to Santa Paula and had brought his TV-radio repair business with him. He retired some years later. The other sad event was the sudden death of my nephew Amador Chavez who died of a heart attack. Amador was one of two nephews and a niece raised by my mother. He had retired from construction work a few years earlier and lived in Santa Paula with his wife, Hortencia. They had five grown sons—Robert, Larry, Rickey, Danny, and Paul. Also,

Naomi got injured at work. She was sitting on a wooden chair during one of the classes, and fell to the floor when the chair collapsed, which caused a hip and shoulder injury.

I continued to work for the same company and also stayed involved in the church, the schools, and the community. That year, we finished building a two-story educational wing at our church. It was dedicated that same year. Most of the men from the church worked on the building, which consists of a social hall and four classrooms on the second floor. It was actually quite a lot of fun as we worked together in fellowship.

The year of 1984 brought some new experiences. First, I lost my bid for a third term as a school board trustee. State assemblyman Jack O'Connell had supported my campaign by walking a precinct to distribute my flyers. Jack was eventually elected as a California state assemblyman where he served for several years. As of this writing, he is still California's Superintendent of public schools.

Secondly, Patricia left her position at Itel Corporation and to work as Associate General Counsel for New United Motor Manufacturing Incorporated (NUMMI), which is a joint venture between General Motors and Toyota. The company had just been organized, and Patricia was the only woman in the original management team that launched NUMMI in 1984. The operations were set up in the vacant General Motors plant in Fremont, California. Among other responsibilities, Patricia was responsible for the financing of the newly-acquired machinery used for assembling automobiles. Several years later, Patricia became vice president of legal, government and environmental affairs, human resources, and corporate secretary. NUMMI was a $4.5-billion automotive manufacturer with approximately 5,700 employees. Her work required her to travel extensively throughout the United States and to Japan. Patricia also became a board member of the public radio and television station, KQED, in San Francisco.

While at home, I was surprised by the school district professional staff who hosted a retirement dinner for me at the Port Hueneme Officers' Club. After dinner, several speeches were made recognizing my service to the Santa Paula Elementary School District. I was presented with three prints sketched by a local artist. I had never heard of a school board trustee honored in such a way.

To date, I treasure those gifts, and I am most grateful to have been honored by such wonderful people. Naomi, on the other hand, had to retire from her job because of a disability associated with her injuries from the school accident.

During this time, my son Paul had asked me if I could get him a job with the company I was working for so I got him a job as an apprentice operator. The union agreed to accept him as an apprentice. He worked with me as an oiler. An oiler is a man who works with a crane or a large backhoe operator to give signals and maintain the machine. One time, he got mad at me and walked away from the job, and went to call one of his friends to pick him up. Before he could make the call, I went over and convinced him to come back, and he did. He learned really fast how to operate a large backhoe and other equipment. But then, one day, he decided to go up north to Oakland. There, he got a job working for a Lucky Grocery Store and lived with Patricia.

In 1985, I continued working for the same company out of Camarillo. I worked Saturdays quite often and sometimes even on Sundays, which made for a good paycheck. I was also involved in the History and Archives Commission of the conference of our church.

On the health front, I had been having trouble with my prostate and on Tuesday, June 11, 1985, I had prostate surgery, which kept me off work for three weeks. While I was still convalescing, Naomi and I went on a trip to the East Coast. Our pastor at the time, Josue Mora, took us to the airport. On Tuesday, July 2, we took a flight to Baltimore with a change of flight in Louisville, Kentucky. When we arrived in Louisville, we went to a restaurant in the airport oblivious of the time change and when we came to the boarding area, we found out that our plane had taken off. We managed to get another flight an hour later but the destination was Washington DC, not Baltimore. When we arrived, John was waiting for us in DC. When we didn't arrive in Baltimore on the originally scheduled flight, he had a hunch that we had missed the flight. After investigating, he learned that we were on the flight for DC. John was working at an office in Fort Meade, Maryland. He lived in nearby Hanover where he had bought a house.

We arrived on Tuesday, and on Wednesday, we drove to Annapolis. Then, we went to Baltimore where we had dinner on the waterfront. On Thursday, July 4, we visited Fort McHenry and in the evening, we watched a spectacular show of fireworks at Fort Meade. On Friday, we drove to Williamsburg, Virginia, and then to Yorktown and Jamestown. We went to the Washington Naval Shipyard Museum on Saturday, walked the mall and then visited the NASA (National Aeronautics and Space Administration) Space Museum. On Sunday, we went to church and then to the Aberdeen U.S. Army Museum. We visited the White House, monuments in the Mall, and Arlington Cemetery. On Tuesday, we drove to Pennsylvania and through York, Lyon, and Lancaster on our way to Gettysburg where we drove around taking pictures of the many monuments and cannons left from the Civil War. On Wednesday, we drove to Annapolis, walked around, had dinner, and returned home. On Thursday, we spent the day just resting and on Friday, we flew back to Los Angeles via Louisville and Indianapolis. On Tuesday, July 16, I went back to work. The rest of the year, I campaigned for a city council candidate and, later on, for my third try at the school board—an election I lost as I mentioned earlier.

On March 26, 1986, John and Mary had their second child, a daughter named Renee Nicole. Meanwhile, Patricia had met Eric Klein, who worked for a NUMMI chemical supplier as a chemical engineer. They fell in love, and got married on June 1 of that same year. The ceremony took place at Green's restaurant on the waterfront in San Francisco at Fort Mason. Both sides of the family were present. The ceremony was a typical Jewish wedding ceremony. That same year, Patricia became a member of the board of trustees of Mills College, her alma mater.

On July 31, Naomi and I took a week off from work to meet our new granddaughter on the East Coast. We took our younger son, Paul, with us. John's house was a two-story house, and we slept in the master bedroom, which was upstairs. The following morning, Naomi was coming down the stairs and tripped on her own gown. She fell down four stairs and landed on the floor. She passed out, and it took a while for her to regain consciousness. She hurt one of her hips and a shoulder although by the next day, she seemed okay.

On that trip, John rented a mid-size RV, and we decided to drive all the way to the state of Maine. The first day, we drove to Boston and from there we drove to nearby Mendon to visit Mary's parents, brother, and sister. While there, we went to a dinner at the place where Henry Wadsworth Longfellow lived and wrote some of his poems. We stayed overnight with the Sawyers, and the next day, we headed up north. We drove along the coast and stopped at Salem to visit the witch houses. From there, we drove through Lexington. When we got to Norwalk, Connecticut, it was late in the evening; and we stopped at McDonald's to buy some coffee. Naomi and I were asleep at the time. John was driving and Paul was sitting in front with him. When John gave Mary her coffee, she took it and sat behind the front seat on an icebox that contained our cold drinks. When John took off with a sudden jerk, the icebox slid back and Mary's hot coffee spilled on her stomach and legs, burning Mary pretty badly. We rushed her to a nearby hospital, and the doctors told John that Mary would need to stay there at least two days for treatment of her burns. Since there was nothing else we could do, we left her in the hospital and continued up north to Kennebunkport where we stayed at a park. John kept in contact with Mary, and on the way back, we picked her up and drove back to John and Mary's home.

On the way back, John decided to drive through New York City so we drove the RV down Broadway with people staring at us, wondering what the heck we were doing driving an RV through downtown New York. We drove all the way to the waterfront where we parked to have dinner. That evening, we saw what nightlife was like on the waterfront. There were drug dealers, pimps, and prostitutes doing their business in cars parked nearby. Paul was sitting in the front seat by the door, and was scared to death—in fact, he had a large crescent wrench in his hand waiting for someone to kick the door open. Those that came by the RV thought we had prostitutes ready to do business. It got so bad that we had to pull out of there and continue on our way home.

It was a short vacation but other than Mary's unfortunate accident and a couple of fifty-dollar fines for transporting a butane tank through a tunnel and over a bridge, the trip turned out to be very interesting, to say the least. Mary continued her treatments at home. Before we left, John took us back to Gettysburg so Paul could see it firsthand. We were back home by August 9 and back to work. That year, our new pastor, Reverand Ariel Zambrano, received his PhD from Claremont School of Theology. Also that year, two of our dear church members passed away—Mrs. Alejandra Gonzales on July 9 and Mr. Leo Ramos on October 2, 1986.

The year of 1987 brought new additions to the family. First, Daniela, our second grand-daughter, was born at Alta Bates Hospital in Berkeley, California on February 20 to a girl Paul had dated in Oakland, California. The baby was initially raised by the girl's mother. Naomi and I had met the girl at Patricia's wedding. Paul was still going out with her then. We didn't see the baby until years later when she was around five years old. On July 13 of 1987, Patricia gave birth to her first child who was a baby boy named Elliott Drew Klein. He was also born at Alta Bates Hospital in Berkeley, California. Naomi went to be with Patricia during Elliott's birth and was in the delivery room when the baby was born. I received a call from Patricia herself about an hour after delivery to let me know that she was doing fine and to tell me about Elliott. That same month, Jonathan visited us for a few days. I didn't meet baby Elliott until September 5 when Patricia came to visit us. We met them at the airport, and I remember holding the little fellow in my arms as he slept soundly.

During Patricia's pregnancy, Eric and Patricia had thought about opening a restaurant, so they developed a business plan. That same year, they bought a small restaurant in a very good location near the Claremont Hotel in Berkeley and turned it into a Mexican taqueria The taqueria was named Viva! Taqueria. Eric started the operation, and they covered their liabilities from day one.

Eric had his own job as a chemical engineer, so they decided that they needed someone to manage the restaurant full-time. At that time, my youngest son, Paul, was working at a grocery store in Oakland. He quit the grocery store job to work at the restaurant, which he eventually began to manage. Paul was doing well with the restaurant and wanted to open another one in the area, but it was not the time. Patricia had just bought a large home in a gated community in Lafayette, California and was not ready to invest in another restaurant. Paul lived with Eric and Pat. By this time, I was a supervisor and stayed very busy at work and in my volunteer activities at church and in the community. I sang in the church choir on Sundays and often was called to be a speaker.

Nephew - Amador T. Chavez

Chapter XXXI

RETIREMENT AND TRAVELS ABROAD

When 1988 came around, I was thinking of retirement and decided that this was the year. I hated to leave the best construction job of my life, but my body was telling me that it was time. The years I had spent operating heavy equipment, as much as I loved it, had taken a toll on my back. I told my employer well in advance that I would retire by July. It meant my last day of work would be on Friday, July 19, 1988. The next day, a party was organized at a park in Moorpark, California and I was thanked for my years of service to JFJ Engineering Incorporated. Among my retirement gifts was the traditional gold watch, which I continue to wear. Naomi was present and so was my daughter, Patricia, who had come to be with me. I made a speech thanking my employers for allowing me to work for them for the past ten years. A few days later, I sent them a formal thank you letter expressing my appreciation for the years I was privileged to work for them. This was unusual in unionized construction work, but I am a very conscientious person.

Meanwhile, Paul had taken over Viva! Taqueria and was actively managing the restaurant. He was doing a good job as the restaurant kept very busy. A Bay Area newspaper gave the restaurant a good review saying it was one of the best Mexican food restaurants in the area. Paul had the personality to deal with his customers and worked to ensure that customers were pleased with the food and the service.

In October of that same year, Naomi and I flew to Oakland on the first leg of a nineteen-day European trip. On Saturday, October 1, 1988, Eric,

Patricia, Elliott, Naomi, and I boarded a plane at San Francisco Airport bound for Dulles Airport where we would transfer to a Paris-bound flight. We had our first experience with an aborted takeoff. Just as the plane was about to lift off, doing about 150 miles per hour, the pilot suddenly slammed on the brakes and reversed the engines, coming to a complete stop. It was a scary experience! The pilot then explained that a window had flown open in the cockpit. The bad news, he said, was that the brakes got really hot from having to stop so suddenly and that we'd have to wait around forty-five minutes before we could take off again so the brakes could cool off.

Our seats were not the best because we were sitting in the center rows with a bulkhead in front of us. We left at 7:00 p.m. and arrived in Paris at 7:00 a.m., the next day. We found Charles de Gaulle Airport to be a modern facility. After getting off the plane, we rode on an escalator for a long way. We found out that while escalators are convenient, they can also be dangerous. When we got close to the passport checkpoint, we noticed that the area was very crowded, and that there was no room for people to get off the escalator. We became worried that we would all bunch up on the escalator. There was a panic for a moment until we were able to jump off the escalator by pushing our way through the crowd that was standing up against the escalator.

After we retrieved our luggage, we left the airport and rode a bus to the metro, which took us to the vicinity of the Notre Dame Cathedral where we got off and found a restaurant to have breakfast. As we rode the metro, we noticed there was graffiti just like we have here. After breakfast, we went to a hotel that turned out to be an excellent hotel. Small rooms but immaculate.

The next day, we walked about a mile to the Notre Dame Cathedral. We were in awe of its size and architecture. As we entered the cathedral, there were signs that warned us to watch for pickpockets. From there, we walked another mile or so to the Louvre Museum where we got to see many famous paintings and Roman, Greek, and Egyptian sculptures. I thought it would surely take us at least two days to see all the paintings and sculptures. And, of course, we couldn't miss the *Mona Lisa* which was beautiful. We didn't get to see everything but I did enjoy what we were able to see. We also enjoyed the sidewalk restaurants.

The next day, we rode the metro to the Champs-Élysées. From there, we walked to the Arch of Triumph, which was being restored at that time. Eric and

I went up to the top where we enjoyed a beautiful view. We could see how all the boulevards came together at one point, just like the hub of a giant wheel. After lunch, we took the metro to the Eiffel Tower. What a massive structure! I had seen it before during the war but this time, Patricia and I took the tram to the second level, and what a breathtaking view of Paris! From there, you could see in every direction and as far as the eye could see. The city of Paris went on and on. It would have taken at least a year of going out every day to fully experience this great metropolis. I found many of the streets to be very narrow and many of the buildings to be very ornate. You could tell that they were very old. Most of the buildings had gargoyles.

On a Wednesday, as much as we hated to, we left Paris from the Gare de Lyon at 11:45 a.m. on a fast train that was very comfortable and smooth. We were bound for Avignon where we arrived around 4:00 p.m. The countryside, as seen from the speeding train, was green with many small farms. We passed many colorful towns with very old buildings, the kind of buildings that give character to a town. Our only brief stop was at Lyon, which is a very big city. We stayed overnight in Avignon, a walled city with many outdoor restaurants. At night, we strolled to the Palais des Papas, a huge church built before the fourteenth century and which is still in use. We learned that this part of Avignon served as the papal city during the fourteenth century.

We left Avignon the next morning at 8:30 a.m. We rode a train to Nîmes, a town that had just experienced a flood a few days before during which twelve persons drowned or so we were told. We had breakfast there, and changed trains to Nordone, our next stop. From there, we went to Portbou at the Spanish border. There, we changed to a slow train bound for Barcelona. We arrived in Barcelona at 5:15 p.m. That night, we had dinner at La Costa Brava restaurant and stayed at the Ronda Hotel in Playa Paja. On Friday, we got up late, had breakfast and strolled along narrow streets. We did some shopping and walked to the Ramblas, a wide promenade with all kinds of vendors and many thieves as well. We walked all the way to Plaça de Catalunya, and from there, we walked to the Picasso Museum. We also walked to a park by the zoo and, from there, to the waterfront where we saw a replica of the ship *Santa Maria*. We went back to the hotel after a tiring day.

We saw a lot of graffiti in Spain. On Saturday, we took a forty-five-minute train ride along the Costa Brava to a coastal resort named Pineda del Mar. The beaches were beautiful with clean white sand and many outside restaurants all along the coast. The average taxi ride cost us 480 pesetas ($4), and our hotel cost $90. We discovered, as we tried to do transactions at the bank, that two languages were used—Catalunyan and Castellano. The streets, plazas, and buildings were named in both languages.

Many of the streets in Spain, like in most European countries, are narrow and one-way. Cars were parked wherever they could squeeze in. Sidewalks, at that time, were about two feet wide if there were no cars parked on the sides. On the main street, the parking was more uniform.

We found ordering food to be a problem. You had to get used to what they had to offer as opposed to what was on the menu. I remember one night during dinner, Naomi asked for iced tea, and the waiter didn't know what she meant. He went and consulted with the cooks, and pretty soon, he came back with a cup of hot tea and a glass with ice.

On Sunday, we left Barcelona at 11:00 a.m. The train ride was excellent, but after going through Tarragona toward Zaragoza, we were asked to change seats because we did not have reservations. The countryside was plain and it reminded me of the New Mexican desert. There were many one-room buildings built from rock, and every once in a while, we would pass train stations that looked like they had been abandoned for many years. There were also scattered windmills that reminded me of *Don Quijote*. The Ebro river ran along the train route for a long way. Soon, we began to see orchards of apples, peaches, grapes, almonds, and olives. We reached a small town named Atalayud, and from the train, you could see an old Moorish temple on a hillside. From there, there was nothing else but hayfields all the way to Madrid.

After getting off the train in Madrid in the evening, there was an escalator which took passengers from the train platform to the train station which was a floor above. When we got to the moving escalator, Naomi, who had a Gucci purse hanging from her right shoulder, got on the escalator, which was very crowded. She was about ten people ahead of me. When I got on, a young man wearing a checkered pull-on sweater pushed me and the people in front of me to one side as if he were going after someone. It turned out that he was. He stopped next to Naomi, and as I looked up, I saw Naomi pull his sweater up from his waist and retrieve the wallet that he had taken from her purse. She turned back and yelled at me, "He tried to steal my wallet!" The guy just froze next to her. As soon as they reached the top, he took off with me in pursuit, but he went out the front door of the train station and disappeared into the night. Naomi told us later that she had felt a tug on her purse, and immediately knew what was going on.

We took a taxi to Hotel Serrano where we had reservations. The area where we stayed was the modern fast-paced part of Madrid. The following day, Monday, October 10, we took a taxi to El Prado Museum, but it was closed. So we walked to Plaza del Sol then to the old Madrid section. We had refreshments at the Plaza Mayor; then, we took a bus back to the hotel. In the afternoon, Naomi and I took a bus tour of Madrid. On Tuesday, we went to El Prado Museum again and very much enjoyed the works of Goya, El Greco, and Velasquez, among others.

In the evening, my son-in-law, Eric, and I went to make reservations for a night sleeper train to Lisbon, Portugal. The next morning,we went to el Rastro (flea market) near La Plaza Mayor. It turned out to be a market for junk, clothing and leather goods. At 10:30 p.m., we left by train for Lisbon. We were on the last coach (a sleeper couchette), and our tiny sleeping compartments were the last two available couchettes.

At midnight, we heard a loud pounding on our door, which scared the heck out of us. We, in turn, pounded on Eric and Pat's compartment to wake them up before we dared open our door. When we did, three men told us we were crossing the border into Portugal. They asked us for our passports, which, they said, would be returned to us upon our arrival in Lisbon in the morning. We gave them our passports with a bit of concern, but they turned out to be legit government personnel.

As the signs of a new day started to emerge, I decided to get up as I was tired of bouncing back and forth in my bunk all night. I went outside to the outer aisle to look through the window at the passing scenery. All I could see were olive orchards all the rest of the way. When we started to come into Lisbon, I began to see many shacks and shanties where poor people lived and grew their own vegetable gardens. They reminded me of the poor people of Barcelona who lived in makeshift houses made of bricks along the railroad tracks.

We finally arrived in Lisbon at 9:30 a.m. We took a taxi to the Hotel York. As the taxi took us through the waterfront, I began to get the impression that Lisbon was indeed a very old city. All the buildings and monuments looked old and were covered with a dark film of soot. The traffic was slow—nobody seemed to be in a hurry. The hotel where we stayed that night was on a narrow street. The buildings in the area looked very run-down, but when we went inside, they were actually very elegant. In the afternoon, we went to lunch and window-shopped. It was raining, so we went from building to building and walked up some narrow streets to a cathedral that was built in the fourteenth century. Then, we continued walking up to Castello de S. Jorge. On Friday, we took a train to Nazaré, a village by the sea.

On the train, our luggage was stacked on the vestibule of the car. There was a fellow wearing a sweatshirt with a hood over his head so that all you could see were his eyes. He told us not to worry about our luggage. I told Naomi, "I hope that when the train slows down, he doesn't start throwing our suitcases out and then jump out himself." We laughed but with a bit of suspicion. As it turned out, he was a very helpful individual who helped us unload when we arrived. When we arrived at Nazaré late at night, an old lady was advertising two rooms for rent. It was very dark and we had no idea where to go so we agreed to rent from her since she said her house was just two blocks away from the beach. We all piled into a very small taxi, and the old lady sat on my lap as we drove to her place where we stayed for two nights.

The following morning as we walked on the beach, I noticed many old women dressed in black with huge mustaches like Pancho Villa's. Nazaré turned out to be a quaint and beautiful village. The fishermen, who were mending their nets, wore black pants and shirts. The story we heard was that in the fourth century, a monk brought a statue of the virgin from Nazareth which was a small community of fishing families said to be descendants of the Phoenicians—thus, the name Nazaré. It is supposed to be one of the most photographed fishing villages in the world. Fishing boats rolled back and forth as the waves came in and out. We were told that in the past, families would help pull the boats onto the beach. Then they began to use oxen to do the pulling but they were now using tractors. The older men and women continued to use the traditional dress—black Phoenician caps, shirt and trousers for the men, and black dresses for the women. Nazaré had many curio shops. Many buses came during the day loaded with tourists. There was an abundance of fine restaurants. We spent most of the day, Saturday, just walking around and shopping for souvenirs. At 4:15 p.m., we boarded a bus for Lisbon. Along the route to Lisbon, we saw a beautiful countryside and many small villages. That night, we lodged at Princereal Hotel.

On Sunday morning, we had breakfast on the top floor of the hotel with a view of the city. We then rented a car and drove to Évora, an interesting walled city of forty-five thousand inhabitants. That night, we stayed at a posada. The next morning, we walked through the city and took many pictures of the narrow streets and a Roman Temple (believed to have been dedicated to Diana), which was destroyed in the fifth century. The Moors took possession of Évora in the early eighth century until they were driven out by Afonso Henriques in the twelfth century. Many kings lived in Évora from time to time. Casa de Osos is a temple where a monk, we were told, used the bones of five hundred padres to line the walls and pillars of the temple.

After shopping and having a delicious lunch of lamb chops, we returned to Lisbon via Setúbal, a port city with many poor people. We drove up a hill to the Pousada de Castelo de Palmela, which is an old castle on top of a hill. The castle had been transformed into a posada and restaurant which overlooked the Bay of Setúbal. After dinner there, we continued on our way to Lisbon. We crossed the bay via a bridge that looked like the Golden Gate.

On Tuesday, it rained all day, and we just stayed in the hotel until the afternoon. Then, Naomi and I went for a stroll along Avenida Libertad, which is the main street in Lisbon. Just a block away on a side street, we saw black families living in squalor. What a pitiful sight! In the evening, we had a delightful dinner at the hotel's top-floor restaurant. On Wednesday, we got up early and used three taxis to take us to the airport, which was very congested. We used three taxis because Patricia had seven huge boxes full of dinnerware and all kinds of artwork that she had bought. On the way, the taxi driver asked us where we were going. We told him, "To California." He said, "With all the earthquakes there, no way would I like to go there."

At the airport, I told Patricia, "It'll cost you a fortune to ship all those huge boxes." But, to my surprise, they checked them in, and it didn't cost her a nickel more. To board the plane, all the passengers had to get on a large bus with security guards hanging all around it. They took us to the plane and made sure we were on board. I felt uneasy, wondering, *Why all the guards?*

The flight took seven and a half hours to New York. It was a tiring flight, but we were glad when we landed at JFK Airport where customs was a breeze. However, we had to wait five hours for our flight to San Francisco. We left on a 747 jet at 6:00 p.m. and arrived in San Francisco at 9:15 p.m. PST. We were all happy to be back home safe and sound. The next morning, it felt good to talk to people who understood us and to eat the food we were accustomed to. That morning, I ate a tortilla with gusto. That afternoon, Naomi and I had the pleasure of attending our first World Series game ever. We went to see the last game of the series, thanks to our daughter, Patricia, who had access to tickets. That was the year that the Dodgers beat the Oakland A's in four straight games. At that time, I had no reason to hurry back home since I was retired.

When we returned to Santa Paula, I continued in my many activities both in the church and in the community. I also became a member of the Hispanic Mission Evangelism Committee. The Hispanic Mission was a new organization within the California-Pacific Annual Conference of the United Methodist Church. Its role as a ministry was designed to help existing Hispanic churches within the conference improve their ministries and start new ministries by training ministers as well as lay missioners.

During the following year of 1989, I began to get accustomed to getting up late in the morning—no more getting up at 5:30 a.m. in order to be at work at 7:00 a.m. I was still very busy with church and community work. In August, we again flew to Baltimore for a few days of vacation and travel. John had made plans for all of us to go by car to the south this time. The first night at John's house, my nephew Steve Pineda, who was on the East Coast, dropped by to visit John and his family. The following night, we met him again in Baltimore where we went to watch a baseball game that was between the Orioles and Boston.

The next day, we were on our way to the south. That day, we traveled through Virginia, the Carolinas, and into Georgia. By late afternoon, we were in Atlanta. We rode around a bit before stopping at a motel for the night. On our way to the motel, we were on an eight-lane freeway, and a guy in a motorcycle passed us going at a high rate of speed. Suddenly, we saw a semi-truck about a quarter of a mile in front of us, and it was throwing sparks from underneath. As we traveled a little closer, we saw the motorcycle fellow lying in the middle lane of the freeway. Lucky for him, a big rig stopped just in front of him as he lay on the pavement. Then, we realized that the bike had hit the semi from behind. The guy must have jumped or fallen off from his bike as it hit the truck. When it did, the bike got caught under the semi, and the driver didn't realize what had happened. We sped up and caught up with the semi and motioned the driver to stop. He stopped and so did we. When we told him that he had a motorbike caught underneath his truck, he couldn't believe it until he got down and saw it. We went to bed wondering what happened to the motorcycle driver.

The next morning, we headed for Florida and stopped in Orlando where we went to Disney World. There, we met Steve Pineda and his family again. I remember that we had dinner in a Moroccan restaurant. The next day, we left for Miami. While there, John, Mary, and the kids went swimming at the beach while Naomi and I went window-shopping along the beachfront stores. While in Miami, Mary got a phone call with the sad news that her father had passed away. That brought sadness to all of us.

We left Miami and drove north. On the way, we stopped at Cape Canaveral; and nearby was a community called Pineda, which we found interesting. Our next stop was St. Augustine, supposedly the oldest city in the United States. We spent some time walking around and doing some shopping for souvenirs. From there, we continued north, and spent the night in a small town. The next morning, we stopped at Savannah, Georgia. As we drove into the city, we noticed trees with dangling moss. We stopped at a park, which had a bronze statue of John Wesley. Across the street was a big church, and we went in. A lady gave us a tour explaining that it was the church where John Wesley preached while in Georgia in the 1730s. We also went to the riverfront and found Savannah to be a very beautiful southern city. From there, we drove straight home to Hanover, Maryland. Once home, Mary left for Massachusetts to be with her family.

That year we spent Christmas at Lake Tahoe where we would spend many more holidays. In February of 1990, we spent a weekend in Donner Pass Lodge and enjoyed the snow. That same week, I served three days on jury duty in the Ventura Courthouse. Otherwise, I stayed busy in my church. Also, a group of men from our church went to help with the restoration of the Barsdale United Methodist Church. We regrouted the rock foundation that had deteriorated.

In July, I was invited by the Hispanic Mission director to go to Atlanta, Georgia, to take a course on church congregational development at the campus of Emory University. Two pastors and I agreed to attend the training course. We left on July 8. After two weeks, one of the pastors decided to go home, so I asked if my wife could come and fill in for him. They approved and Naomi came and we enjoyed the classes together. While there, we had the opportunity to visit the Martin Luther King Jr. tomb and the Ebenezer Baptist Church. We also visited the Jimmy Carter Library, the Atlanta underground, and other surrounding landmarks. We were back home by August 10, the day before our wedding anniversary.

A week later, our grandchildren Jonathan and Rene came to visit us for a week. That became a busy week. We took them to Disneyland, Magic Mountain, the county fair, and the beach. When they left, we let out a sigh of relief.

Chapter XXXII

THE UNEXPECTED SECOND CAREER

I had become a member of the Hispanic Mission Council of the United Methodist Church's California-Pacific Annual Conference. The Council's role was to provide oversight and direction to the Hispanic Mission ("(HM"). The role of the HM was to create programs that helped Hispanic churches develop new leadership and new congregations. The HM was inaugurated on September 18, 1988, during a very impressive ceremonial service officiated by Bishop Jack M. Tuell at the Wilshire United Methodist Church in Los Angeles. A minister was installed as the executive director of the HM.

Three years later, in July of 1991, the bishop met with the council and informed us that the HM executive director would not be reappointed to the position. The council viewed that as a problem for us as Hispanics. The bishop said that we could hire another director if we wanted the Hispanic Mission to continue and we indicated that we did want it to continue. The council didn't know quite what to do, so Mr. Clifford Aguilar, Chair of the Council, unexpectedly asked, "Al, would you be willing to take over while we find someone?" He caught me by surprise because never in my wildest dreams had I ever thought of having the opportunity to function in an executive director role, with an office and a secretary who would expect me to tell her what to do. I didn't know what to tell him but I was mindful of the urgency of continuing the ministry. Finally, I said, "I'll think about it."

During a meeting that followed, Clifford said, "Al, you have a lot of experience in church work. I'm sure you can handle the position." I then spoke before thinking and said okay. I would start on a part-time basis and hold the fort until someone could take over the position. The plan was for me to take the position with the understanding that by the first of the coming year, a full-time person would start.

On July 12, I officially took over the office except that two days later, I had to travel to the Perkins School of Theology at Southern Methodist University in Dallas, Texas, for a two-week seminar on Hispanic ministries. When I returned, I went straight to work on July 30. I had committed to working three days a week. The HM office was located in a church in Long Beach, California. The Spanish-American Institute had its offices upstairs in the same building. My office was just one room. It had two desks, one for the secretary and one for the executive director; a computer; a copier machine; and a conference table for eight people. Clifford Aguilar, Chair of the Council, was also the director of the Spanish-American Institute. That was a great help for me because if I needed advice, I would just run upstairs and meet with him. He was a lay person with a great deal of experience in the United Methodist Church. He had served for many years in leadership roles for the church worldwide. He was one of, if not the most, influential Hispanic lay leaders in the United Methodist Church. He had chaired committees in different divisions of the General Board of Global Ministries (GBGM). I had known Clifford for a number of years but not very well. Nevertheless, I had a great deal of respect for him.

After getting acquainted with the few files that were left in the office cabinet, I began to think about what my priorities should be at the HM. There was an issue that needed to be dealt with right away, and that was the traditional Labor Day family camp that was coming up at the end of the month. Brochures announcing the camp program had to be developed and mailed to all the Hispanic churches. Scholarships were to be offered, and a program had to be developed for the three-day camp. I immediately called a meeting of people who had been interested in the camp program in past years. We were able to develop a program, and select a theme for the camp. Flyers and applications went out to the churches. That was my first hurdle. That was a hectic week, and I was beginning to learn quickly that there was no such thing as a three-day part-time job.

The following week, I took the ideas that had accumulated in my mind over the last two weeks, and began to write down some goals. I concluded that there was a critical need in our Hispanic churches for the training and development of lay leaders. Taking into consideration that I was to be in this position only until the end of the year, I wrote a set of goals that could be completed by the end of the year. I would (1) meet with all the district superintendents, share my goals, and enlist their support; (2) visit all Hispanic churches and meet with the pastors to invite their cooperation; (3) select a group of four clergy who could develop practical courses of study for lay missioners; (4) develop a timetable for length and frequency of studies; (5) organize a cadre of academia instructors and a committee of academia advisors; (6) develop a model for pastor-mentors; and (7) identify areas where lay missioners could be of service once trained and certified by the academia.

I had no problem organizing a team for curriculum development. Those agreeing to help were my former pastor, Dr. Ariel Zambrano, Dr. David Tinoco, Rev. Antonio Fernandez, and Rev. Francisco Canas. By early November of that year, all my goals were completed except for one. Praise God for that! Six syllabi for courses on Christian education, evangelism, Bible survey, homiletics, church history, and basic fundamentals of the United Methodist Church were developed. Later on, courses on pastoral care, church administration, and national plan modules were added to the curricula. Each course was designed to be taught in fourteen hours, two hours per session once a week. Two different courses would be taught every week.

In late November, I received a call from Dr. Roy Barton—director of the Mexican-American Program of the Perkins School of Theology in Dallas, Texas—asking if it was okay to use our courses of study as one of two modules in the training of church instructors. I said "yes", and was invited to make a presentation in Dallas regarding our Academia Hispana. In December, thirteen clergy and one layperson volunteered to serve as academia instructors, each choosing their own field of expertise. We organized a service of consecration for the instructors and invited Bishop Jack M. Tuell to the Pico Rivera United Method Church where he consecrated all thirteen persons as the official instructors of the Academia Hispana. A few days later, one of our district superintendents told me that the bishop was very pleased with the service at Pico Rivera. Shortly after, another clergy was added to the group of instructors.

In late December, I went to San Diego to organize a district Hispanic task force, which would meet monthly, to discuss the district Hispanic ministries and how we could work together to improve and develop new ministries. District Superintendent George Walters helped me organize the task force and also wrote letters to the churches in El Centro, Brawley, and Calexico requesting them to send representatives to the newly organized task force. In Los Angeles, Rev. John Green invited me to visit his church in Watts. He walked me through a part of the neighborhood, which was mostly Hispanic. I told him that as much as I would like to start a ministry there, I didn't have a person or the resources at that time to do so. I was also working with Dr. Don Locher to find a pastor for El Mesias United Methodist Church in Pacoima. The church was in dire need of a pastor.

As far as classes were concerned, my advisors and I set January 1992 as the date to start the academia classes. One of my greatest concerns was the dwindling numbers of ordained clergy in our conference. I saw some challenging years ahead as several ministers were reaching the age of retirement. I felt that we needed to develop incentives to recruit Hispanic youth into a career in the ordained ministry. We had been forced, so to speak, to bring clergy from other denominations, which set our congregations back in their understanding of our philosophy and system. That was why Academia Hispana needed to play an important role in the development of leaders for our congregations. We agreed to charge a ten-dollar fee registration. I called Joaquin Garcia, Director of the Diaconal Ministries in Nashville, Tennessee, asking for certification of our courses of study. He wasn't in, but returned my call later on. I explained to him what I wanted. He told me to send him a copy of the courses with a letter explaining our program and our request. He also told me that he would get to it as soon as he got my materials. He would also see if he could arrange for a consultation with the directors of the General Board of Higher Education and Ministry and the Claremont School of Theology.

At this time, there was jubilation and sadness in our family. We were jubilant because our daughter, Patricia, had been elected to the board of directors of Levi Strauss& Co., the apparel conglomerate based in San Francisco. The sadness was due to the passing away of one of my half sisters, Dolores "Lola" Zavala, who had made it possible for me to come to California. She had also been responsible for helping my oldest brother, Manuel come to Santa Paula way back in 1935. Lola's family consisted of her husband, Pedro; sons Alfred, Eddie, Robert, and Reginald; and daughter, Virginia, who were all married.

Ironically, at work, I felt a great sense of excitement and satisfaction because things were moving forward quickly and I was working full-time. I would drive to Long Beach and stay at Motel 6 for two nights a week, and on the other days, I would go to meetings from home. Whenever I went out of town, Naomi would go with me. At the office, I got a letter from Kattia, my secretary, saying that she was going to attend a college in Albuquerque, New Mexico, and would be leaving by December 30. I was so busy meeting in different churches that I really didn't think about being without a secretary.

I started a scholarship fund for students attending the course of study at the Claremont School of Theology. Long Beach superintendent Sharon Rhodes Wickett donated the initial amount of three hundred dollars. The pastor of Santa Paula's El Buen Pastor United Methodist Church pledged one hundred dollars a month to the fund. Reverend Ruben Saens verbally announced that he would donate five thousand dollars to the fund, and I told him that if he would, we would name the fund in his honor—but his pledge never materialized. Rev. Leo Nieto wrote me a letter asking that I investigate the reasons for the reduction in scholarship funds for the local pastors' course of study at Perkins School of Theology. I called some of the members of the Conference Board of Ordained Ministry, and no one knew how much the conference was supposed to contribute.

When January 1992 came around, I was still the HM executive director with no signs of anyone else coming to take over, so I kept on making plans. We started the first quarter of academia classes at the El Sinai United Methodist Church (United Methodist Church will hereafter be referred to as "UMC") in Anaheim, La Trinidad UMC in Los Angeles, and El Buen Pastor UMC in Santa Paula with a total of forty-five students. Two additional classes were slated, one in May at St. Luke's UMC Highland Park and another in August at Nestor UMC in San Ysidro, California.

By virtue of my office, I became a member of the board of directors of the Southwest Regional Training and Resource Center (SWRTRC), which met twice a year in Phoenix, Arizona. This organization was represented at three conferences—Rio Grande, Desert Southwest, and California-Pacific.

Each conference had three representatives—a staff member, a clergy, and a lay member. The SWRTRC was financed by the General Board of Global Ministries of United Methodist Church, and its purpose was to provide training for clergy and laity on leadership and other facets of the church. As I visited churches from Indio to Calexico and San Diego, I sensed that people thought the HM executive director had the answer to all their problems and needs. The job could have been overwhelming if I had allowed it to be.

On occasions, I translated materials for conference staff members as a gesture of mutual cooperation. I also continued recruiting prospective lay missioner students for the classes that we were offering. I wrote articles for publication in our conference paper, *Circuit West*, letting readers know of the opportunities to become lay missioners. Lay missioners were laypersons who were trained in different areas of ministry so they could start small Bible study groups in their own churches. The strategy was to eventually bring community people without a church into the church. Our philosophy was "Three out of five people you pass by in the street do not attend a church." They were the people that we were targeting for the Bible studies.

In the city of Pomona, California, we started a new congregation with Dr. Ariel Zambrano as a part-time pastor. Dr. Zambrano was a retired clergy to whom I am indebted for his staunch support of my ministry.

I had a Nazarene pastor who called me persistently almost every day. He wanted me to find him an appointment to a church in our conference. In fact, I used to receive regular calls from pastors of other denominations, from pastors who lived in Mexico and from pastors of other Methodist conferences as well. Somehow, they thought that I was the person that made pastoral appointments to local Hispanic churches. Actually, all I did was ask for their résumés, make copies, and share them with our bishop and the cabinet members.

I also became a frequent speaker in Hispanic churches explaining our ministry work. As I became more confident of my ministry, I made plans for a possible consultation with the Claremont School of Theology and some of the leaders of the church's General Board of Higher Education and Ministry as Joaquin Garcia had suggested. I wanted to discuss the possibility of validating our academia courses of study. I wanted our courses of study to be approved as a requirement for licensing of students entering the seminary course of studies. I spent most of my days going to meetings. I met with pastors of local churches to determine whether I could be of any help. Also, once a week, I would drive to a central point in Los Angeles to have breakfast with small groups of pastors to discuss ways of doing ministry together.

As Vice-Chair of the Conference Board of Evangelism, I had to attend the conferences as well as meetings of the HM Council. I traveled quite frequently to Dallas and San Antonio, Texas, as I was asked to lead training sessions for general agencies of the church. Matters of budget and funding for our work were always before us. We were continually trying to explain to the higher-ups the importance of our work. With the limited funding that we received, somehow, I kept things moving along. In all my running around, I always found time to stop and visit my other half sister Lucy who was well into her eighties and lived in Huntington Park, California.

By the spring of 1992, I had brought into reality, with the help of some of my supportive clergy, a set of academia courses for lay missioners. A consultation took place, and our academia was eventually approved as a licensing school for those seeking the local pastor route. Also, a ministry program in Spanish for local pastors was established at the Claremont School of Theology.

By August, we had six classes for lay missioners throughout the conference with sixty students in attendance. Selected clergy took turns teaching classes that fell within their expertise; and in May 1993, thirty-eight lay missioners, both men and women, graduated. At least six of them eventually became local pastors. I also organized ministry task forces in every one of the mainland districts. Funding for the HM continued to be a problem, but I continued to work with much enthusiasm. In fact, during the session of the 1993 annual conference at Redlands, California, I stood up and told the presiding bishop and the assembly that I would continue as director of the HM without a salary. All I wanted was to be paid for my travel expenses while away from home.

At the end of the conference, the bishop set up a Blue Ribbon Committee to study the ministry of the HM and to issue a report the following year. After many meetings and consultations with the members of the HM Council and me, the Blue Ribbon committee reported the following year that the HM was a vital ministry and should continue. The committee further proposed that the HM office be housed in the conference headquarters building in Pasadena, California, and that it be a part of the Conference Council on Ministries (CCOM). They indicated that the HM executive director should be a member of the CCOM staff with the title of associate director of the CCOM. The conference voted in favor of the recommendations and made them effective, January 1, 1994.

Chapter XXXIII

NAMED TO A CONFERENCE STAFF POSITION

With the same old murmurings by some Hispanic clergy that the position should be held by a clergy, I continued with the new position and a beginning salary of fifty-two thousand dollars a year plus travel allowance. A new secretary was hired, and I was on my way as a new member of the conference professional staff. So, again, I entered a new world, so to speak. The good thing was that while the rest of the staff members had portfolios that included more than one ministry, my portfolio was focused only on the Hispanic ministry. However, I did belong to other conference committees that required my involvement in and out of the conference and had several leadership responsibilities at my own church. I would travel sixty-eight miles each way from Santa Paula to Pasadena and back five days a week and oftentimes more. Somehow, I managed.

I soon adjusted rather well to the new position, and things were proceeding smoothly with the HM ministry. I had a couple of lay missioners working in local churches developing congregations. I would have them work so many hours per week, and pay them an hourly stipend. We had two classes of lay missioners studying a couple of modules provided by the church's National Plan for Hispanic Ministries.

Chapter XXXIV

ELECTED TO GENERAL CONFERENCE

During the 1996 annual conference, I submitted my name as a candidate for delegate to the United Methodist Church's General Conference, the body that develops the rules and policies of the church worldwide. When the voting started and later reached the fourth round of voting, I didn't think I had a chance of being elected. But at the end of the eighth round of voting, a young woman and I were elected. When I saw my name on the screen, I went numb. I didn't know what to think.

After several meetings for newly-elected delegates, we were ready for the conference to be held in Denver, Colorado, from April 16 to 26. When the conference started, I began to learn about the politics of the church and the lobbying that goes on. Representatives of different church organizations had signs and pamphlets that they handed to delegates as we went in to the convention hall. They were trying to persuade delegates to vote for issues that their organizations wanted passed. I had heard so much about the general conference of our denomination, and now here I was a delegate. It was a great privilege for me because I knew of only one other Hispanic layperson that had ever been elected. This time, there were two of us—a clergy and myself.

Ethnic minority caucuses held receptions after the conference sessions were over in the evenings to advocate for legislation that would benefit their group's cause. The invited keynote speaker for my first conference was Hillary Rodham Clinton. She impressed me with what she had to say. She received a standing ovation from those in attendance. By virtue of being a delegate to the general conference, I automatically became a delegate to the Western Jurisdiction Conference. Several of our bishops were elected at that conference. It was at that conference that I really learned a great deal about church politics. When the voting started for the election of bishops for certain conferences, the candidates who didn't get a certain percentage of votes in the first round of voting were automatically eliminated. It was interesting to watch the different caucuses holding impromptu meetings to strategize for their candidates or to establish support for a second-choice candidate.

Chapter XXXV

ELECTED TO THE GENERAL BOARD OF GLOBAL MINISTRIES

In the midst of voting for our candidates for bishop, I was greatly surprised when a clergywoman, who was one of my staunch supporters as director of the HM, came to me and asked if she could submit my name for election to the General Board of Global Ministries ("GBGM"). I didn't know much about the GBGM, but I said okay. A greater surprise came to me when she came back and told me that I had been elected to the GBGM as one of the directors representing the Western jurisdiction. The GBGM is the body that carries out the mandates of the general conference throughout the world. The board is made up of ninety clergy and laity. It meets twice a year, once in the spring and once in the fall. I was to serve a quadrennium.

The first meeting I attended was held in New York City; and at that meeting, the decision was made to hold subsequent meetings in Stamford, Connecticut.

Chapter XXXVI

TRIP TO GERMANY

The following year on May 25, 1997, I took a vacation with my daughter and her family, my son Paul and his daughter, and Naomi. We flew to Frankfurt, Germany, to visit our oldest son, John, and his family who lived in Mannheim. The day after we arrived, we rented a van and all went for a ride to Schlierbach, the village where I spent the rest of my Germany occupation days after the war.

The next day, we drove to the Rhine River which we crossed on a ferry to a place where we boarded a cruise boat for a four-hour trip on the Rhine. We enjoyed seeing castles on the hillsides and vineyards planted along the steep mountainsides. The next day, we drove south; and on the way, we stopped at Rotenberg, an old German town preserved from ancient times. From there, we stopped at Augsburg where the U.S. Military Intelligence headquarters was located and we took some pictures next to some 155 mm cannons on display that were just like the ones I fired during WWII.

From there, we continued to Munich and after an overnight stay there, we visited the former concentration camp at Dachau. After our visit to Dachau which was an unforgettable and sad experience, we drove to Garmisch and stayed overnight at an American-run hotel for military families. It rained most of the time. The following morning, we left to visit beautiful Neuschwanstein Castle on top of a mountain. We stopped at the village below, and after lunch, we took a horse-drawn wagon up the hill to the castle. It was one of the most impressive castles I have ever seen. The view from the castle was breathtaking. We stayed in the village hotel that night, and the following morning, we drove back to Mannheim, stopping at Heidelberg for dinner.

The next day, we drove back to Heidelberg and walked through the beautiful old town. That night, we boarded a riverboat for a three-hour river cruise. We had dinner on board. As night fell, we saw the lighting of a castle with fireworks, a great spectacle that happens four times a year. The remaining time in Germany was spent going for walks through paths that went through farms and forests.

Our trip back was uneventful, and once I was back at home, I resumed my duties and busy schedule.

Chapter XXXVII

CONTINUATION OF GENERAL BOARD OF GLOBAL MINISTRIES

Those elected to the GBGM are assigned to different committees. I was assigned to three different committees—the Finance Committee, the Missions Committee of which I was vice-chair and the Peace with Justice Committee. In the Finance Committee, I was appointed to the Audit Subcommittee, which met once a year at the GBGM headquarters in New York City. I learned a great deal about how the denomination spends money for ministries around the world. Through the Missions Committee, I learned about the mission work of the church worldwide; and through the Peace with Justice Committee, I learned quite a bit about our prison systems—especially how special interests that build prisons want to keep building more prisons, and once they are built, how they need prisoners to fill them up to justify the costs. The church's interest in our prison systems is in the welfare of the prisoners and providing chaplains as a way of counseling inmates.

The GBGM is made up of people from all over the world. Every time we met, we got a pulse of what was happening around the globe and developed international friendships. Serving the church on a global and national level exposed me to many new and exciting experiences.

On one occasion, I was one of two directors who were sent to a European consultation that was held in Vienna, Austria. We were there for about five days. There were representatives from Germany, Italy, Russia, and other countries.

In the evenings, some of us would take the subway to a cathedral, which seemed to be in the center of the city. One time, three of us went to dinner and window-shopping. When we got to the cathedral, there were vendors selling concert tickets so we bought tickets for a concert. We went to hear a string ensemble play and sing the music of Tchaikovsky.

On another occasion, I went with a group of German clergy to hear an organ concert at the cathedral. The clergy spoke nothing but German. I couldn't understand what they were saying or laughing about. Once in a while, suddenly realizing that I couldn't understand them, they would speak a few words in English for my benefit. Nevertheless, I enjoyed their company. The concert at the cathedral was somewhat boring for me and what made it worse was the uncomfortable wooden bench we had to sit on.

After the concert, we stopped at a restaurant for dinner where there happened to be a German minister who was able to speak English with me. Even though I couldn't understand the jokes that were told in German, I had a good time with them.

The consultation in Vienna had been about the work of the United Methodist church in Europe. I enjoyed Vienna very much, and my only regret is that I didn't get to see the Danube River nor the Vienna Woods. Someday, perhaps, I'll go back.

On another occasion, two of us global ministries directors were sent by the Missions Committee to Atlanta, Georgia, to a reception for retiring missionaries. We heard many interesting stories about their work in Africa and other parts of the world. We were given the commission to pin retirement lapel pins on each of the retiring missionaries. Naomi went with me, and she made some friends while there. Later on, a group of us directors were invited to go to Franklin, Louisiana for a week to help with the work at the United Methodist Church center warehouse. The center distributes emergency aid wherever there is a catastrophe in the world. We went to help pack kits for different types of emergencies. At the end of the week, we took a day to go on a boat to explore the bayous in the area before leaving for home.

In general, the board meetings were held in Stamford, Connecticut and we stayed at the Westin Hotel. The meetings started on Monday at 2:00

p.m., and Naomi and I used to arrive on Saturday. On Sunday, we would take the train to New York City, which was about an hour away, and go to a Broadway show.

My work at the conference was going well. I received the Harry Denman Evangelism Award, which was a great honor for me. At home, many things were also happening. Patricia kept us informed of her career. She was becoming a professional board member of very prestigious organizations. During the year, she had become a board member of the California Manufacturers' Association, a trustee of The James Irvine Foundation, a trustee of the RAND Corporation and, as mentioned before, a member of the Mills College Board of Trustees. At New United Motor Manufacturing, Inc, she had become, Vice President of Legal, Environmental, and Government affairs and Corporate Secretary. She is an exceptional woman who is always showered with honors.

Chapter XXXVIII

PASSING OF LOVED ONES

During the month of July 1997, my oldest half sister, Luz, or Lucy as she was known, passed away at a hospital in Huntington Park, California. Her death left a void in our lives because she had always been concerned about her brothers and her family. She was always praying for our welfare. My brother Tony and I took care of the memorial service for her in Santa Paula where she was laid to rest.

That same year, my son John and his family returned from Germany to Maryland. My sense is that the move was a big move for John's children who had to adjust to a new life in the U.S. with new friends.

During the latter half of 1998, Naomi complained of discomfort and vomiting associated with a bloated stomach. Looking back, she suffered tremendously that year. Her doctor thought the problem might be due to neuropathy of the intestines which he said diabetics like Naomi sometimes experienced. After much suffering by Naomi, our daughter, Patricia, insisted that Naomi's doctor conduct further tests at our local hospital. Unfortunately, the tests indicated the presence of a mass. The doctor called Patricia to tell her that they wanted to schedule Naomi for surgery first thing the next morning. He said they would not know whether the mass was benign or malignant until a biopsy was conducted.

On December 17, my poor wife Naomi was scheduled to undergo surgery. My children and I held hands with Naomi and prayed for her before she went in to the surgery room. As Naomi was wheeled into the surgery room, I, along with my children and members of our extended family went into a family room where we all continued to pray as we waited. After a much longer wait than anticipated, her surgeon came in and told us he had removed a massive cancerous ovarian tumor. What should have been only a two hour surgery ended up being a five hour surgery that was very complicated because of the size of the tumor and the fact that it had wrapped itself around her other organs. He also told us that the tumor was very sticky and that he had only been able to remove about 95 percent of the tumor. At that point, I could not control my emotions, and turned away from everyone to cry. The woman who had been part of my life for fifty-five years was in bad shape. After she became conscious and was made aware of her situation, I remember her saying, "I have a long haul ahead of me." And she did.

During surgery, her surgeon performed a colostomy which Naomi found upsetting and unpleasant. Naomi's incision from the surgery took months to heal because as a diabetic she did not heal easily. In fact, the surgeon had to order a newly-invented machine that was attached to Naomi's incision which helped it heal by extracting blood and bodily juices from the incision area.

That following year, Patricia and I took Naomi to her chemotherapy and doctor appointments. There were times when the doctor would tell us that she was progressing, only to be followed in the succeeding weeks with news that the count was high again. My work schedule was very heavy during the first months of 1999 but, fortunately, Patricia came for every chemotherapy treatment and had made arrangements for full-time live in help prior to Naomi's return from the hospital.

I had a lot of traveling to do and had to go to my job every day. That was the pace I kept until the day of my planned retirement, June 30, 1999. At last, I would be able to spend more time with my ill wife. On the day of my retirement, I was honored at a beautifully planned reception at St. James United Methodist Church in Pasadena, California. It was a wonderful event. People walked into the reception room where a pianist played soft beautiful music. There were decorated tables with finger foods and fruits for everyone to enjoy as they visited with each other. Bishop Roy I. Sano and other church dignitaries were present including my daughter, Patricia, and my son Paul.

Although we had a constant caregiver for Naomi during the day, it was my responsibility to care for her at night. It was then that I began to understand how hard it is to take care of a bedridden patient attached to different machines. I learned that it takes a lot of patience to care for an ill person. There were many times when I had a hard time trying to convince Naomi that she could not get up and walk. With all the painkillers she was taking, she kept thinking and insisting that she could get up and go to the bathroom by herself. Whenever I took her to the hospital for a checkup, I would take her for a ride to see the countryside, trying to distract her for just a few precious moments from her continuing pain.

As I mentioned before, visits to the doctor were moments of hope, only to find out later that there was no reason for hope. She wouldn't say anything and my heart ached for her. The only strength we had was our faith in God. It was heartbreaking for me when she would call out to me and say, "Honey, make this pain go away from me." It gave me such a helpless feeling. I couldn't stand it to see her suffer.

After a few months, I decided that I needed to get away from the house for a few days, so I asked my son Paul to go with me to spend a weekend in Puerto Rico. I don't know why I chose Puerto Rico. Maybe I chose it because I had been there before with Naomi. Patricia stayed with Naomi while I was gone. When we got to Puerto Rico, Paul and I rented a car and drove across the island to a beautiful lagoon on the western side where we rented a boat. We went snorkeling which is something I had never done before. From there, we returned to Viejo San Juan and visited a fortress I had visited previously. I have many friends in Puerto Rico, but didn't feel like visiting anyone.

We returned home after three days. That year, I also completed my four years as a director of the General Board of Global Ministries. However, I was still on the board of the Southwest Regional Training and Resource Center. Through this organization, I was able to bring leadership training to our conference churches and to pastors in the northwest part of Mexico. Bishop Elias Galvan, who had been chair of the board for many years, was transferred to Seattle, Washington and I was elected to take his place as chair of the board. I continue to serve in that capacity as of this writing. After my retirement, I was invited to join the retired Hispanic clergy chapter which I did. As a layperson, it was an honor.

My son Paul had started his own salsa and guacamole factory in the Bay Area. He was living with his girlfriend, Priscilla Miranda and had finally decided to get married. He chose the backyard of our house for the ceremony so his mother could be present. It was a bittersweet moment. All the immediate family on both sides were present. Later on, Paul and Priscilla had a more formal wedding at the church. Rev. Jose Vindel, pastor of El Buen Pastor United Methodist Church, officiated at both ceremonies.

In November of 1999, my brother Tony and I went to Puerto Rico representing our conference's Hispanic caucus at the National Hispanic Caucus MARCHA's annual meeting. That happened to be the year when officers were elected. At the meeting, my name was submitted for president, and the name of a clergywoman was also submitted. She won by one vote. Then, my name was resubmitted for vice president, and I was elected.

During our stay on the island, my brother Tony, another delegate from our conference, Mr. Nelson Mendez, and I took a bus to Viejo San Juan. From the bus station, we took a trolley that took us through the narrow streets of San Juan. At one point, we got off to go souvenir shopping and as we walked around the cobblestoned streets, we noticed that Tony was falling behind. We waited for him to catch up. When he did, he said that he felt very tired. His face was very sweaty so we decided to go back to the hotel. The next evening, he and others walked a couple of blocks from the hotel to the beach. Later, he told me that he had felt dizzy. The following day, we left for home. When we got home, he went to see his doctor, and was told that he had experienced a serious heart attack. He was sent to a hospital in Thousand Oaks, California and after a few days, was released pending further testing. On January 31, 2000, he was taken to Santa Paula Hospital and was placed in the intensive care unit. The following day, I went to see him, and he looked good after a rough night. We talked for a while, and prayed together before I left.

The next morning around 8:30 am, I got a call from my niece Emily and she told me that Tony had just passed away. I immediately called my oldest brother, Manuel, in Texas and let him know. I drove to the hospital and was allowed to see Tony before they took him away. My brother Tony and I were very close, so his death left another sad void in my life. He was well-known and liked in the community for he had served on the City Parks and Recreation Commission and had served as a Little League umpire for many years. He served his church with devotion and was an excellent lay speaker. I was very sad to have to say good-bye to my brother and close friend.

At home, Naomi continued to be very sick. On May 9, 2000, she was admitted into the local hospital to determine whether she was suffering from other complications to her internal organs. An ultrasound and other tests showed that she had an abscess in her liver. She was given antibiotics to fight the infection. After a very difficult struggle with the infection, she finally came home on May 15. We had an excellent hospice nurse who did everything she could do to help Naomi. We appreciated her efforts very much. The woman who had been serving as a regular caregiver to Naomi got a steady job and recommended her sister, who, to the end, did a splendid job as Naomi's caregiver. Fortunately, Naomi was blessed with excellent caregivers. She was also blessed with regular visits from her family and the extended family of our church. And, of course, our children regularly visited their mother. John came all the way from Maryland, and Patricia and Paul from the Bay Area.

I continued to take Naomi to the doctor in Ventura and for short rides although she no longer seemed to enjoy them. Her pain kept torturing her, and she would often ask for a Vicodin pill to alleviate her pain. Sometimes, she would stare at me without saying anything, and I would wonder what was going through her mind. On July 26, she had a very bad night. Her breathing was hard and difficult. We thought that she wasn't going to make it through the night, so we called her brothers and sisters, but she made it. The following day, she looked very listless and by evening, her breathing began to falter. At 10:30 p.m., she stopped breathing with our children and me by her bedside.

At that moment, I felt so alone without her. The woman who had given me three lovely children and who had shared her love with me to the end was gone.

It became very hard for me to live alone with objects around the house that reminded me of her. Weeks later, my children and I planted a rose garden in her memory at El Buen Pastor United Methodist Church, the church where she had been active all her life.

Later on, we also dedicated a Carillon Bell System at the church in memory of her, her parents, and my brother Tony. I continued visiting my children and grandchildren in the Bay Area. I would also go and do minor repairs at the family restaurant in Berkeley. I stayed involved in the church, both locally and regionally. On one occasion, I was invited to Washington DC for a drug abuse workshop. While there, a clergy friend and I took the opportunity to visit the mall and some of the museums including the White House. That same month, I attended the Hispanic national caucus meeting in Elizabeth, New Jersey. At that meeting, new officers were elected.

On Thanksgiving Day, my children and all of Naomi's side of the family met at my brother-in-law Sam Salas's home for a turkey dinner as we had done for many years before. Just before Christmas, I bought some trees to plant in front of the church, also in memory of Naomi.

On December 23, Patricia, her family, and I left on a flight from San Francisco to Oaxaca, Mexico, where we spent Christmas. We thought it would be best to celebrate the first Christmas without Naomi away from Santa Paula. We arrived and stayed at a hotel located on a hillside where we could see the city of Oaxaca. On Christmas Eve, after a special dinner, we went to the zocalo to see the Festival de los Rabanos (Radish Festival). In the plaza, there were displays with beautiful figurines of people and buildings carved from radishes. It was quite a unique display of art. Then, later in the evening, there was a Parade de los Rabanos.

During our three-day stay, we also went to see the Rufino Tamayo Museum, the home of Benito Juárez, and the State Anthropology Museum. We also went to see the ruins of Monte Albán and other historic sites in nearby towns. From the city of Oaxaca, we took a flight in a small charter plane to the southern coast of the state to beautiful Huatulco. Upon arriving at the Hotel Real, we were met by hotel waiters offering us a glass of orange juice. All along that part of the coast, we saw great hotels with huge swimming pools. The streets were lined with coconut trees. Lodging and food were great at the hotel. On the morning of New Year's Eve, we left on a flight to Mexico City where we boarded another flight via Guadalajara to San Francisco, California. It was a great vacation.

Upon returning to Santa Paula, I heard the news that my niece on Naomi's side of the family, Pamela Kennedy Luna, had given birth to a baby girl whom they named Vanessa Nicole. Back home, after catching up with my mail, I sent a letter to our bishop with a list of suggested names of possible candidates for the post of district superintendent as recommended by the Hispanic caucus LAMAG. Of all the district task forces for Hispanic ministries that I had organized, the only one remaining active after I left the Hispanic Mission was the one in my district, which was the Santa Barbara district. In June 1999, I was recommended to be a member of the conference's Board of Ordained Ministry, and was accepted and have served since with my term ending in 2007. This is one of the most important boards of our church conference.

In February 2001, my son Paul opened a branch of his Gente Foods business here in Santa Paula, and I became involved in managing the office. I also became secretary of Gente Foods Corporation. On June 10, I went to the retirement celebration of one of our clergy in Huntington Park, California and during the reception, my niece Dora Reyes, introduced me to a group of ladies who were sitting at our table. During the conversation, one of the ladies, whose name was Lydia, needed a ride home. Since it was on my way home, I offered to give her a ride. That led to a friendship that eventually turned serious. We started communicating by phone, and I took her out to lunch a couple of times. Then on one occasion, I took her for a ride to show her the vineyards north of Santa Barbara, which she enjoyed a great deal. I kept seeing her often.

In August, I went with Patricia and her family on a two-week vacation to Spain. We flew from San Francisco to Munich, Germany and connected on another flight to Madrid where we spent a couple of days. We then flew to Málaga where we rented a van and drove to Granada where we stayed two days. From there, we drove to Seville where we went sightseeing in a horse-drawn carriage. While in Seville, we visited beautiful gardens and managed to attend a concert with Spanish Flamenco dancers.

After two days, we drove to beautiful Torre Molinos by the south coast. Our hotel was by the beach with a breathtaking view of the Mediterranean Sea. While there, we went to see a bullfight one afternoon. After returning the van at Málaga, we took a flight to the island of Mallorca where we stayed at a new Marriott resort. There, we rented a car and visited Palma, which is the main city of the island and then drove over a mountain range through beautiful villages. From Mallorca, we took a flight to beautiful Barcelona.

While in Barcelona, Patricia and I went on a comprehensive tour of the city. On another day, we went to have lunch and walked along the ramblas—a long wide walkway with many vendors and one—person entertainment shows. It is also a place where pickpockets abound. While there, a man came up to me and extended a newspaper in front of me while asking for *monedas* (coins). Meanwhile, behind me came his wife who stuck her hand in one of my front pockets. Luckily, I felt her hand, and pulled it out and told them to get lost. They ignored my scolding and kept asking me for money. I made myself scarce. It is an interesting place to visit as long as you are aware of the thievery that goes on, especially when you are in a crowd.

We continued to walk the narrow streets and window shop. After a couple of days, we flew back to Madrid and stayed at a hotel a few blocks from El Prado Museum. While there, we visited the museum and a nearby flea market where we bought some small antiques.

From Madrid, we flew back to Munich and, from there, back to San Francisco. During that vacation, I flew on five different planes. We were able to cover a lot of territory by flying. My last flight was from San Francisco to Burbank. It was a very enjoyable vacation.

Back home, I continued to see Lydia; and after some time, I took her to meet my daughter and sons. They all liked her and so did Naomi's brothers and sisters. They all realized that at my age I needed a companion.

*Anneliese Klein - daughter of Eric
Klein and Patricia Pineda*

*Grandaughters - Daniela Pineda, Renee
Nicole Pineda and Anneliese Klein*

My Children - Paul, Patricia and John

My son-in-law Eric Klein, Patricia and
daughter-in-law Mary Pineda

Albino, son Paul, daughter-in-law Priscilla and
Naomi at Paul and Priscilla's wedding

Paul and Priscilla' - Wedding

Niece - Dora Reyes and Sister -
Luz T. Chavez

My Family: John, Naomi, Paul,
Patricia, dad Albino

Late Brother - Antonio, Patricia, Dora

Grandson - Jonathan Pineda   *Grandson - Elliott Klein*

Chapter XXXIX

MY SECOND MARRIAGE

On April 27, 2002, Lydia and I were married at El Buen Pastor United Methodist Church in Santa Paula, California—my home church for most of my life. After a week's honeymoon in Hawaii, we settled at my home. Lydia is from El Salvador, Central America. She is a naturalized American citizen. Her English is very limited. She is a very out-going and compassionate person who makes friends easily. We have our cultural differences now and then, but generally, we get along fine. A few months after our wedding, she went to visit her relatives in El Salvador, and the following year, we made arrangements for her older sister to come visit us.

Lydia has a very interesting background. She came to the United States some sixteen years ago via the desert but got caught and was deported to Mexico where she was jailed for being an undocumented person. After a week in jail, she was set free with other people, and had a rough time getting back to her country. A few years later, she tried it again and finally made it to Los Angeles with the help of a coyote. Being an industrious person, she got jobs cleaning houses in the West Los Angeles area, and people liked her because she is a meticulous and a hard-working person. When she does something, it has to be right. She is very sure of herself.

Two years after she arrived in Los Angeles, she applied for and received her green card for legal residency. A few years later, she took the citizenship test and passed it, thus becoming a naturalized American citizen of which she is very proud. Many wealthy people she worked for liked her. In fact, one of her former employers was our maid of honor at our wedding. Later on, she came to visit us, and we enjoyed a nice lunch together.

I have told Lydia that when I finish my story, I would like to write hers. As I continue to travel, Lydia always goes with me. During April of 2003, I went with her to El Salvador to meet her relatives, and they all liked me. I enjoyed the country, but noticed poverty everywhere we went. The only thing I couldn't stand was the humid tropical climate. Also seeing guards everywhere, including on delivery trucks, made me feel insecure and afraid. The only place I felt somewhat secure was at the Holiday Inn where we stayed. Besides visiting her many relatives, we managed to take a couple of tours to some of the ruins, which I found very interesting.

Before marrying Lydia, I had been working to develop a ministry in the central California town of Shandon. After Lydia and I married, we both worked there every other weekend. She was a great help working with the children. Unfortunately, we were unable to continue, but we do visit the church from time to time.

During the year of 2003, my daughter, Patricia, and her family and mother-in-law; my son John and his wife and son; and Lydia and I flew to Guanajuato, Mexico to spend the Christmas holidays in the beautiful colonial town of San Miguel de Allende. While there, we made side trips to Querétaro, Guanajuato, and Morelos. We enjoyed a wonderful time there.

Lydia and I spent as much time as we could during the winter at Patricia's house in Tahoe Donner just north of Truckee, California. Lydia had never seen the snow before, so for her, it was quite a novelty. Lydia is a devout Christian and a very compassionate woman, and as I mentioned before, befriends people easily. She has become a leader in our church where she has endeared people. She has become the chairperson of our church's Evangelism Commission. I continue as chair of the church's administrative council and, also, as chair of the board of trustees. Very likely, this is the last of my years of tenure in these responsibilities. It is time for the younger people to take charge.

The year 2004 kept me busy going to meetings both locally and out of town. In May, Lydia and I flew to Baltimore where we visied my son John who lives in Fort Meade. While there, my son took us for a tour of Baltimore and Annapolis, which are always interesting places to visit. During the last day of June, our pastor, Rev. Jose Vindel, was appointed to a large church in San Bernardino, California. We now have a new pastor, a woman, who is handicapped and uses a mobile wheelchair. Our church is adjusting, and so is she. In August, Patricia, her family, Lydia, and I spent a week in Puerto Vallarta, Mexico. Upon our return, Patricia gave the church a power point monitor in honor of her aunts Toni Kennedy, Estella Russell, and Tita Vargas.

In the first part of November, Lydia went to El Salvador to visit her family while I went to Milwaukee, Wisconsin, to a meeting of the National Hispanic Caucus MARCHA. I was gone for four days, and on my return, I left for Lafayette to visit my daughter and her family.

That year, we spent Christmas at Patricia's home in Lafayette, California, and stayed home for the New Year. My right knee had been giving me a lot of trouble and was hurting. I had gone to the University of California Medical Center in San Francisco and two orthopedists who saw me suggested surgery even at my age given my good health. Patricia inquired about surgeons in Ventura County (where I live) who specialize in knee surgery. A knee doctor from Ventura was recommended, so I went to see him. He also recommended surgery given the worn out state of my knees.

On January 3, 2005, I was admitted to St. John's Hospital in Oxnard, California and on that day, underwent surgery on my right knee. I was out of the hospital five days later with a therapist giving me knee therapy at home. Two days after returning home, an acute stomach ache hit me. I was rushed back to the hospital. After two days of extensive testing, I was told that my gallbladder was badly infected and that I needed surgery right away. On January 11, my gallbladder was successfully removed. I remained in the hospital until January 16 and then went home. Thereafter, knee therapy was no piece of cake. After home therapy stopped, I had to go to a local clinic to continue with my therapy. Therapy sessions were something I dreaded, yet I had to do it religiously. Every time the therapist tried to bend or press my knee down, I felt like screaming. I would yell, "Stop!" Today, over a year and a half after, my knee still hurts; and worst of all, my left knee is so painful that I have a tough time getting up from a chair. I lose my balance easily, and I can't do the things I was accustomed to doing. Painkillers don't help much, and I don't want to have surgery on my left knee. I guess I'll have to tolerate pain for the rest of my life. In spite of it all, I continue to stay active. I drive to Los Angeles regularly to attend church related meetings and I regularly work in my garden in addition to engaging in all the other activities I'm involved in. I guess my situation is not so bad since I am in my 80s.

In spring, we were saddened by the death of two dear persons from our church. First, our former pastor of many years Dr. Ariel Zambrano passed away in March; and then in April, a dear church member, Ms. Julia Huerta, who had been among the most faithful servants of our church also passed away. She had been the church's organist, pianist and music director for many years. She was also a devoted member of the church for most of her life.

In the month of June, Lydia and I went up north to attend the high school graduation of my grandchildren Daniela and Elliott. Every time I see them, which is often, I'm amazed at how fast they are growing. Then, there's Anneliese, the baby of the family. It seems like just yesterday she was a baby crawling on all fours. Now, she is a studious young lady in her early teens. Since she learned to read, she has been fascinated with books. It seems that every time I see her, she has a book in her hands. I am very proud of all my grandchildren, including Renee and Jonathan.

In August, Lydia and I took a flight to Albuquerque, New Mexico, to attend the wedding of our other granddaughter who also seems to have grown overnight. Rene is the daughter of my son John. Her brother, Jonathan, is a college graduate who volunteered to go into the U.S. Army. I guess he got the military gene from his father. While in Albuquerque, we managed to visit Santa Fe, Socorro, Mt. Sandias, and other interesting places in the area.

In August, Lydia went to El Salvador to visit her family and in November, she and I went on a guided tour of Italy. I had previously been to Milan, Venice, Florence, and the northern part of Italy. This time, we flew to Rome; and after a day, we took a bus tour to Pisa, Verona, Venice, Florence, and many other interesting towns in between. During the Christmas holiday, we went to New York to be with my daughter and her family. She was living in a small apartment in a ninety-eight floor Trump Building while waiting for the purchase of an apartment in mid-town Manhattan to be finalized. We stayed at a hotel a block away. It was very cold, and there was a transportation strike, which made for a lot of walking. We nevertheless enjoyed it a great deal. On

Christmas Eve, we and several members of Eric's side of the family had a great dinner at a Mexican restaurant. While there, we went on a bus tour of the city, and were given tickets to go see the Broadway show *The Lion King*.

My daughter, Patricia, in spite of the fact that she is a very busy person, is very much and always has been a family-oriented person. She spends every moment she can with her family. They often travel to different places just to be together. She calls me every day from wherever she happens to be. Her job requires her to travel regularly all over the country and Japan. To me, she is a daughter in a million—a very generous and caring person.

The year 2006 was also one of those years that brought sadness to the family and the church with the passing away of my sister-in-law Toni Salas Kennedy's husband, Harold and then, a few months later, Margaret Salas (the widow of my late brother-in-law David Salas). Shortly after, another church faithful member, Mrs. Chonita Echavarria, also passed away.

During the summer, my wife, my son Paul, and I flew to Maryland to visit my oldest son, John, who was getting ready for an assignment in Iraq after having survived an almost fatal bicycle accident the year before. We spent a few days enjoying his company and that of his wife, Mary. Ironically, his son, Jonathan—who is also in the military, was also getting ready for a second tour assignment in Afghanistan. After we said good-bye to both John and Jonathan, we came back home and then packed again for a trip to Dallas, Texas, to visit my oldest brother, Manuel, who I hadn't seen for some twelve years. Not only did I enjoy visiting with him, but I also had a chance to meet most of his adult children for the first time who came by to say hello. Manuel has eight children from his late wife, Mildred. They are Paul (whom I haven't met in all these years), Michael, Gary, Janice, Anita, Linda, Rick, and Karen (whom I have also not met).

On our return back home, I was asked if I would consider being the grand marshal for the local Labor Day parade. Of course, I said that it would be an honor, which it was, riding in a red Corvette waving to the welcoming crowds.

Last year, I conceived the idea of building a monument to honor all the men and women who have worked as farm workers in the Santa Clara River Valley which encompasses the town of Santa Paula at its geographic core. The city of Santa Paula has roots that are deeply embedded in the farming industry. From the beginning of the late 1880s when pioneering farmers began planting citrus trees and other produce in the valley, farm workers worked alongside them performing most of the back-breaking work and have continued to do so through the years as farming in the area has become a multi-million dollar industry. Farmers have become corporations while farm workers (men and women) continue to stoop and pick from dawn to sundown to earn at best poverty-level wages.

Since the community of Santa Paula and the surrounding areas have greatly benefited from the contributions of the farm workers who also help keep local businesses alive, I have concluded that we owe them some kind of recognition. I believe that a monument in their honor is in order. Consequently, I developed an idea for a monument which includes a mural with a roster of names of farm workers from the past and the present. At one end of the mural, there will be a life-size bronze statue of a male farm worker and, at the other end, a life-size bronze statue of a female farm worker stooping down as we see them in the surrounding fields harvesting strawberries. I shared my idea with a member of the Santa Paula City Council, a member of the city planning commission and with the president of a civic organization. All showed great interest in the proposed project.

I took some pictures of farm workers at work and shared them with a renowned sculptor who liked the idea and showed great interest in sculpting the statues. He also took some pictures in the fields and sculpted two small clay figures which he gave to me. The figures are exactly what I wanted. I also fashioned a small cardboard model of the proposed mural and monument to show others. The city councilman, with whom I had met, presented the idea of the project to the city council. The city council named a monument committee consisting of two council members and two city staff persons. We added the planning commissioner and the civic organization president to the committee as well. The committee has worked with me to further develop the proposed project and to find a location. In presenting the proposed project to the city council, I also presented a pledge of fifty thousand dollars as a grant, which I secured beforehand.

The original shape of the monument was modified by the planning commissioner member of our committee who is an excellent designer himself. Instead of a square mural as I had suggested, he redesigned it so the top of the mural is arched, retaining the same measurements as originally suggested. The statues will remain as I originally suggested. The planning commissioner also added some benches, special lighting and an open-gated iron fence around the structure with trees and plants. After three different choices for the monument location were considered, the city council gave final approval for a location along the train station corridor where other monuments are located. A local community foundation has agreed to manage the donations for the project. As of this writing, we are in negotiations with the sculptor who will build the statues. Also, an advisory committee has been established which consists of influential people—including my daughter, Patricia. As I mentioned previously, I secured, through my daughter, the first fifty thousand dollars as a grant from the James Irvine Foundation. There is a great deal of interest by the community in this project. I greatly appreciate all the cooperation I have received from the individuals who have worked with me on the project. They are the two city councilmen, a city council staff person, a city planning commissioner, and a civic organization leader. The target date of completion of the project, as of this writing, is Labor Day of 2008.

On May 28, 2007, I was selected by the local VFW post to deliver the keynote address at the Memorial Day ceremony that takes place at the monument of the Grand Army of the Republic located here in Santa Paula at the local cemetery. It was an honor for me to do so. I believe my comments were well received by those in attendance.

As of this writing, the world is in turmoil. We are involved in a war with alleged terrorists in Iraq and alleged terrorists in Afghanistan. People are dying in those countries every day. At this point, we have lost over three thousand American soldiers, and others are dying as I write. This is a very difficult war to fight. I keep wondering how a terrorist can be identified with certainty. I believe that most people in the United States are ambivalent about or against our involvement in these wars. We started them, and now I believe we are trying to save face at the expense of many lives.

The world's social order has disintegrated; and it seems that every nation, big or small, is experiencing either great dissatisfaction among its citizens and/or some type of unrest and bombings. Here in the United States, our society has deteriorated to the point that one cannot go out for a walk at night in one's own neighborhood without fear of being assaulted. Drugs and crime have infiltrated not only our communities but also our schools as well. It will take a strong and responsible leader to bring this country back to its old values of honesty, respect, compassion, and justice.

Albino and great grandson - Richie Pineda Montoya

John with son Jonathan

Paul, Priscilla and my new wife, Lydia Sanchez Pineda

Brother Manuel's Children: Linda, Anita, Michael,
Manuel, Albino, Janice and niece Dora Reyes

Son John with his grandson Richie P. Montoya

Lydia S. Pineda and Albino

Son Paul with wife Priscilla

Conclusion

Today, as I look back on my life, I think of many "ifs." What if my father had not passed away at such an early age? What if I had completed my formal education? What if my family had not moved to Mexico? And the "ifs" go on. As I try to make sense of it all, quite frankly, I am very satisfied with the way my life turned out. I learned a lot from the poverty I experienced as a child and as a young man. I believe it built my character. It taught me the value of money and the fact that it doesn't come by easily. I was blessed with my loving first wife, for most of my life, and three lovely children who have remained devoted. We have all flourished financially, spiritually and intellectually. And now, I have a second wife who shares her love with me without reservation. What else could I possibly ask for?

As I think of these things, my heart fills with love and gratitude toward God who has allowed me to experience a life of poverty among the poorest of the poor and a life of great comfort and economic stability. I am deeply satisfied in knowing that we reared our three children to be independent, self-reliant, and happy adults. This was achieved with the help of my first wife who unselfishly shared her life with me until her death. Our children were reared in a Christian environment and now, it is up to them to follow the way of life they were taught as children. Early in our marriage, my first wife and I learned to love and respect each other. The love for our children was paramount in our lives, and their love and the love of relatives and friends helped sustain us as we aged.

Stewardship of our finances was always very important since money didn't come easily to us. Naomi didn't want to be just a homemaker—she wanted to be a contributor. As I mentioned earlier, after the children grew up, she began to work as she did early in our marriage. By being good stewards, we managed to accumulate assets beyond our expectations. Our assets would allow us to live in comfort for the rest of our lives.

Naomi and I never reached the point of being pretentious as we were very conscious of our humble beginnings. My only regret is that Naomi didn't live long enough to enjoy the pleasures of a longer retired life together with me and see her grandchildren grow into beautiful young adults. Today, I continue to live in the same modest home with my second wife, Lydia. My children keep in regular touch with me. In fact, my daughter, a busy person with a career, calls me every day to make sure we are all right. She also always inquires about the well-being of the family members on her mother's side. Lydia and I entertain regularly and always invite Naomi's brothers and sisters to join us. My son John, whose home is in Severn, Maryland, has recently safely returned from a six-month military tour of Iraq and is preparing for retirement after thirty-five years of an honorable army career as an army intelligence officer. His son, Jonathan, who is a noncommissioned officer in the Army Special Forces, has also recently safely returned from his first tour in Afghanistan.

Perhaps someday, world leaders will practice the art of negotiation instead of the art of making war. May God help us!

In writing this autobiography, I wanted to impress upon others how difficult life was for the repatriated. I have no doubt that there are many Mexicans today who continue to struggle as much as we did. However, as I grew into adulthood, I learned that struggles are very much a part of life for most people and how we deal with them is what counts. Struggles help us build character. And I believe that a strong character based on honesty, perseverance, a good work ethic, love of family and, above all, a strong faith in God are the essentials to a good and happy life.